1649568

Me

NOV 0 9 2009

Unlocking Your

Cred

How to U

Brighten

A L

Abı

H

THE ROWMAN

Lanham • Boı

Library of Congress Control Number: 2009923220
ISBN: 978-0-7618-4700-7 (paperback : alk. paper)
eISBN: 978-0-7618-4626-0

"Published with the express permission of the owner of the rights,
Creative Education Foundation, Inc, 48 North Pleasant Street, Suite 301,
Amherst, Massachusetts 01002.
www.CreativeEducationFoundation.org

The Creative Education Foundation CEF is the Centre for Applied
Imagination—helping individuals, organizations, and communities transform
themselves as they confront real world challenges. Founded in 1954, CEPF
is the recognized world leader in Applied Imagination. Alex Osborn, an
Advertising Executive and Educator, not only founded CEF, but also
invented Brainstorming and co-founded the ad firm BBDO. His classic
books, including, *Your Creative Power* and *Applied Imagination*, continue
to inspire the work of CEF. To learn more about Creative Problem Solving
contact CEF at (508)960-0000 or visit www.CPSIconference.com.

∞™ The paper used in this publication meets the minimum
requirements of American National Standard for Information
Sciences—Permanence of Paper for Printed Library Materials,
ANSI/NISO Z39.48-1992.
Manufactured in the United States of America.

Contents

Foreword

Your Creative Power is an old friend of mine. I first read it in the original over forty years ago. It is timeless. In this, its new abridged form, it is also timely as a fresh leadership skill tool.

Alex Osborn, its author, was a prolific and exciting thinker, creative and judgmental. He inspired others by practical role modelship and clear, fundamental instruction. I went to school on his teachings. Step by step, I became creative.

As I have grown into the twilight years of my career, the Osborn impact has sustained and its potential shows increasing promise for many others.

I have extolled it separately in the preamble to a book I authored in 1991, The Idea of Ideas. The books challenge a heightened creativity expectation level. They show that we can readily train to daily, superior, vocational skills. They, particularly Osborn, tell us how.

I personally abridged the excellent original three-hundred page Osborn book as a service to my associates. The supplementary anecdotes and reinforcements that the full text offered added sheer enjoyment and convincing evidence.

This shortened version is pure Osborn text. It retains all of his fascinating insights and principles that outline each and every creative fundamental and step that he lived and practiced and wrote of in the interest of stimulating our creative power.

Robert W. Galvin
Retired Chairman, Executive Committee
Motorola, Inc.

ONE

Creativity Examined

THE LAMP THAT LIT THE WORLD
CAN LIGHT YOUR LIFE

"I'm sorry kid—you're fired!" Thus the ax fell on my neck one Saturday at midnight. I gulped and left *The Buffalo Times* for my lodging at a settlement house in the slums. It seems a century ago, but I can still recall almost every step of that heavy-hearted trek.

The next morning I filled a scrapbook with clippings from the Sunday *Times*. I went to the *Buffalo Express* and asked the city editor for a job. He wanted to know how much experience I had. "Only three months," I said, "but won't you please look over these clippings?" He did so.

"They are pretty amateurish," was his comment, "but our police reporter is sick and I will take a chance on you. I am taking it only because in each of these articles there seems to be an *idea*."

That remark put an idea into my head; and that idea has grown on me ever since. No one in college or elsewhere had ever told me about the value of ideas. But here I found that ideas were diamonds. "If ideas are that valuable," I said to myself that evening, "why don't I try to turn out more of them? If a Boy Scout can think up one good turn each day, why can't I think up a new idea each day?" Well, that's how I got started on making imagination my hobby.

Since my newspaper days, my work has been in advertising; and that means in ideas. Starting from scratch I became the head of an organization of about 1,000 people, many of whom were blessed with more inborn *talent* than I. *Whatever creative success I gained was due to my belief that creative power can be stepped up by effort, and that there are ways in which we can guide our creative thinking.*

Although I have steadily stepped up my own creative power, my claim to any right of authorship is not based on my creative record—but rather on my record as a creative coach. It is this experience of helping others use their imaginations that gives me the hope that this book will be of aid to others.

Too often have I heard intelligent people sneer at would-be creators as "nutty" or "wacky"—as "crackpots," as people with "wheels in their heads," or with "bees in their bonnets." Scholars have scoffed at ideas as being worth "a dime a dozen."

Colleges have slighted the creative mind. Hardly any textbooks give creative thought more than a lick-and-a-promise.

Our thinking mind is mainly two-fold: (1) *A judicial mind* which analyzes, compares and chooses, (2) *A creative mind* which visualizes, foresees, and generates ideas. These two minds work best together. Judgment keeps imagination on the track. Imagination not only opens ways to action, but also can enlighten judgment.

You do much to improve your judicial mind. *But what steps do you take to consciously improve your creative mind?*

Although this book will try mainly to show how to step up creative power to enrich one's life, we might take a glance at what ideas have meant in the forward march of mankind; the use of fire, the wheel, the vise, internal combustion engines, farm machinery.

In our own private lives we wait for things to turn out well, failing to make conscious use of our imagination. *With enough creative effort, each of us could find the ideas that would smooth our rocky roads!*

From literary tales, we recall Scheherazade who spun the imaginative stories of the 1001 Arabian Nights. One of her tales was Aladdin and the Enchanted Lamp. Our Aladdin's lamp is the creative power within the reach of every man and woman.

A mother, about to gather the clan for Christmas week, feared that her eight-year-old daughter and five-year-old nephew would be in constant clash. She said to her husband, "We could ward off this bedlam if we could think up the right idea." She buckled down and came up with a plan. She closeted her daughter and her nephew. Before their wide eyes she poured 50 golden pennies into each of two glasses, saying, "This glass, Cynthia, is yours. This glass, Jackie, is yours." She explained that, for each breach of peace, a penny would be taken out of either glass or both. She promised that on New Year's Day, each might have whatever pennies were left.

Then she placed the glasses on a shelf where both could watch. Cynthia and Jackie acted like angels the whole week. A year later, when Jackie arrived for another Christmas at the old homestead, he actually asked his aunt to "put up those pennies again."

Seldom do we put our heads together and say to each other "Now that we know pretty well what the trouble is, let's sit down and think up what we can do. Let's take a pad and make a list of at least 25 ideas that might work"

What we need is a conscious appreciation of the fact that ideas have been, and can be, the solution of almost every human problem. And, here again, we all need to realize this truth: Each of us *does* have an Aladdin's lamp, and if we rub it hard enough, it can light our way to better living—just as that same lamp lit up the march of civilization.

CREATIVE EFFORT PAYS IN MORE COINS THAN CASH

One of the real rewards of creative effort is the steady climb—the greater likelihood of advancement. The head of a big firm decided to retire. He had seven able assistants. When I asked him how he had picked his successor, he replied: "Year after year, one of my aides had sent me frequent memos which usually began, 'This may sound screwy, but . . .!' or 'Maybe you've thought of this, but . . .!' Even though many of his ideas were trivial, I finally decided that he was the one to succeed me because this business would dry up without a leader who believes in ideas, and has the gumption to spout plenty of his own."

One young friend of mine came back from war eager to get into a different line. He knew what firm he wanted to join. He feared that his first interview would spell success or failure. So, instead of applying in the routine way, he spent a week calling on customers of his prospective employer.

At the end of the week he had dug up 10 pretty good ideas. Then he got his interview, during which he modestly brought up the ideas in the form of tentative questions.

His new boss has since told me, "I am mighty glad he didn't just ask for a job in the usual way. I had already made up my mind not to take anyone else. So I would have turned him down if he hadn't shown in our first meeting that he knew how to get ideas."

Happier living is another fruit of increased creativity. High up in our resources of happiness we can place the proved knowledge that we have, in our thinkery, a well-exercised power to think ourselves out of trials and difficulties. Although it is impossible to lift ourselves over a fence by our bootstraps, it is possible—it can be easy—to lift ourselves over life's obstacles by force of our applied imagination.

Creative effort can be an antidote for worry. Worry is essentially a *mis*use of imagination. By driving our imagination into healthful lanes, we can do much to drive away worry and arrive at better health. Eminent psychologists agree that lack of creative effort is often the bottom of mental unrest and nervous upsets.

People can get more fun out of life by making more of their imaginations, but creative effort offers still another compensation: A person can continue to *grow*. Yes, the more creative you are, the more of a person you become. The more you rub your creative lamp, the more alive you feel. The cash rewards of creative effort are plenty; but the more frequent and more fruitful rewards come in the coin of happier living.

ALL OF US POSSESS THIS TALENT

"Who me? Why I couldn't think up an idea if I tried." Chauncey Guy Suits became head of General Electric Research when only 40. "*Everyone* has some hunches," said Dr. Suits. "No one is wholly without some spark. And that spark, however small, is capable of being blown on until it burns more brightly."

And here's what two educators say in *College for Freedom*: "*All* of us have within us some of the divine creative urge." Scientific tests for aptitudes support that joint statement by President Carter Davidson of Union College and President Donald Cowling of Carlton College. An analysis of almost all the psychological tests ever made points to the conclusion that creative talent is normally distributed—that all of us possess this talent. The difference is only in degree; and that degree is largely influenced by effort.

Scientific findings are borne out by the countless cases in which ordinary people have shown extraordinary creative power. The war furnished overwhelming proof. Literally millions of ideas were brought forward by people who never thought of themselves as in any way creative.

"But," you may say, "although those points prove that I have creative *talent*, they don't prove that I have creative *ability*." Yes, there is a difference. *Most of us have more imagination than we ever put to use. It is often latent—brought out only by internal drive or by force of circumstances.*

Suppose that you were sitting here with me on the sixteenth floor of this building, and I were to say to you, "Here's a pad and pencil. Please write down, within one minute, just what you would do if you knew that this building would immediately tumble to the ground as the result of an earthquake." Your answer might be, "I'm sorry but I wouldn't have an idea."

On the other hand, suppose I were to stage that same scene so as to seem *real* to you—by having a good enough actor rush into my office and shout: "*This building is going to fall down within two minutes!*" If you believed him, wouldn't you shout not one idea but many ideas? Isn't it your drive, rather than your degree of *talent*, that determines you creative *ability*?

And yet, the degree of creative talent does vary. Some believe that its intensity depends largely on heredity, others on the environment. In the opinion of Dr. Alexis Carrel, "Imagination and boldness are never entirely due to environment—neither can they be represented by it." It's the old question of the hen and the egg. To my mind, the truth seems to be that imaginative talent stems more from the environment than from heredity—and that its *conscious* use is a far greater factor than either.

There are some geniuses whose lamps *seem* to need no rubbing. Alexander Woollcott and I were college mates. His native brilliance dazzled and perplexed me. I had to rub hard to get any rays at all from my little lamp, while his seemed so big that all he seemed to need to do was brush his sleeve against it. But the more I saw of him throughout his later life, the more I realized that his abounding mental energy was what made him so creatively productive.

A. J. Musselman is another who apparently could not help but spark almost all the time. He invented the coaster brake and hundreds of other new things. After he had made millions out of his ideas, he built a private golf course in Kentucky. To put his links into the public eye, he thought up a weird annual event—a *club-throwing* contest. But, my friend Paul Hyde knew Musselman as a boy in Wichita, and he told me that Musselman, above all else, was a bundle of energy.

Another seeming exception is Clarence Budington Kelland, who in our century, has turned out more fiction than even Dumas did in his. Those who do not know Kelland might think that he is just a bubbling spring—that his creations just flow, with less effort than is needed to turn a faucet. But, on a vacation with Kelland, I was constantly with him except in the morning. While the rest of us dozed or dawdled, Kelland arose from an early breakfast, chained himself to his typewriter, and forced his creative wheels to spin. "How did you get along this morning?" I would ask him. "I got a lot done," was his usual reply. But now and then he would growl, "I wrote and wrote, but nothing I wrote was any good." Yes, Bud Kelland has made his success by living up to the law laid down by Elbert Hubbard, publicist and founder of the Roycroft Shops, some 40 years ago—"the way to write is to write and write and write."

Brains like those may require less motive power. But it is a matter of degree. We who are blessed with less talent have to crank-up our idea-motors more often, and we have to fuel them with more mental sweat.

But no talent is brilliant enough to create without conscious drive.

EDUCATED OR SELF-EDUCATED; OLD OR YOUNG

"If only I'd gone to college, what a person I could have been!" How often that alibi is secretly harbored, and yet there is no evidence that higher education induces creative power. For one thing, colleges almost ignore the subject of imagination.

Those who go to work in their teens tend to pack into their memories the *first-hand* experience which forms the richest fuel for creative lamps. More than that, these youngsters are forced to acquire the *habit of effort* on which creative power so largely depends.

According to scientific tests for creative aptitude, there is little or no difference between college or non-college people of like ages. Winston Churchill was the poorest scholar in his class at his prep school. He did badly in all subjects. In his later writings, he hit a new creative high.

Some who never reached high school have gone far in creative achievement. Lena Himmelstein came here as a Russian immigrant of 16. She built the Lane Bryant business out of her idea that expectant women would like to dress fashionably.

History records that many great ideas have come from those devoid of specialized training. The telegraph was worked out by Morse, a professional painter of portraits. The steamboat was thought up by Fulton, likewise an artist. A schoolteacher, Eli Whitney, devised the cotton gin.

What could be more preposterous than writing music without musical training? Irving Berlin spent his boyhood as a waiter in Chinatown. He never learned to play, except by ear and only in the key of F sharp. Woollcott's highest tribute to Berlin was this: "He can neither read music nor transcribe it—*he can only give birth to it.*"

Many writers have reached the heights without the help of diplomas. Mark Twain left school when he was 12. Dashiell Hammett was thrown into creative work with no literary training. Hammett got himself a job in San Francisco with the Pinkerton Detective Agency.

He wearily kept sleuthing until one day his boss called him in and proclaimed: "Hammett, you will never make the grade as a detective. You are fired! My advice is to take up writing. Your *detective* work has been punk, but your *reports* have been colossal."

Please don't get me wrong. I favor education. *The point is that the degree of one's creative power does not depend upon a degree. This point is stressed because self-confidence is one of the keys to increased creativity.* Those who missed out on college should feel no fear that they were handicapped creatively.

An enemy of self-confidence is a common notion first expressed by Plato. "Experience takes away more than it adds. Young people are nearer ideas than old people." With due respect to Plato, how could he say that while still listening to the 60-year-old Socrates as he spouted ideas so new that they led to his death 10 years later?

If success comes too soon, it may mean tragedy. Such was the lot of Alexander the Great. He conquered Persia at the age of 25, and he had been highly creative in many ways other than the military. After 25, his creativity was paralyzed by vanity. His only new idea was beardlessness, to shave his face so that he might again look as young as when winning the world. How could such creative talent dim and die out so soon? The answer is that his *effort* died first, and as a result, his talent dried up.

Dr. Charles Dorland's analysis of 400 outstanding careers showed that, on the average, creative peaks were reached around 50. But he also found many instances of brilliant creative achievement in the 60s and 70s. The truth is imagination lasts longer than memory, and that we can keep up our creative power, regardless of age, as long as we keep our inner drive in high gear.

In college at the age of 17, it was my good fortune to see much of a 60-year-old grad. At 76, as U.S. Commissioner Plenipotentiary to the Conference on Limitation of Armaments, the record shows he was then more fertile with suggestions than any man half his age. That was Elihu Root.

Thomas Jefferson retired when he was 66. Visitors at Monticello are amazed at the many innovations he thought up from then on.

Among creative scientists, Dr. George Washington Carver, at 80, was still turning out new ideas—so many that more than ever he merited the tribute paid him by the *New York Times* as "the man who has done more than any other for agriculture in the South." An earlier scientist, Alexander Graham Bell, perfected his telephone when 58, and when past 70 solved the problem of stabilizing the balance in airplanes.

Julia Ward Howe wrote the *Battle Hymn of the Republic* when she was 45. But Alexander Woollcott once told me the best writing she ever did was *At Sunset*, which she penned at 91.

Even if our native talent should stop growing when our body stops growing, it would still be true that our creative ability can keep growing year after year in pace with the effort we put into it. W. Somerset Maugham has put his seal on that truth. "Imagination grows by exercise," said he.

Psychologist George Lawton has stated that the mind, at 80, can still be almost as good mentally as at 30. Specifically, when it comes to creative talent, Lawton tells us that although older people are apt to lose some of their memory power, "creative imagination is ageless."

The older we grow, the more we should know. "When our minds are filled with rich and varied experiences,' said Dr. Harry Hepner, head of psychology at Syracuse University, "we discover concepts that would not occur to us when our contacts with life were more limited."

CREATIVE POWER NEEDS
NO IVORY TOWER

America's architecture is being enriched with more and more temples of research. These laboratories are the ivory towers of science. They provide not only equipment but also a climate ideal for concentrated contemplation. And yet, creative scientists would fall short if they created only while in their ivory towers. For example, Dr. Suits of General Electric has stated that he gets some of his best ideas in bed, while flying from plant to plant, or "while staring out of a Pullman window." A. J. Musselman claimed that he gave birth to his coaster-brake idea while speeding down a Rocky Mountain steep—not in a limousine but on a runaway bicycle.

Samuel Johnson may not have been entirely right when he said that anyone could write anywhere, if they would only set themselves to it "doggedly enough."

But it is true that although artists and writers may require ivory towers, ideas can be created almost everywhere.

One virtue of an ivory tower has to do with time rather than place. *If we set aside a definite period for creative thinking we can best lure the muse.* This rule should govern those of us in business. We should "take time out for thinking up ideas—nothing else," said Don Sampson. Too many of us tackle routine first, usually because it is easier. Sampson rightly recommends mornings for thinking, afternoons for routine.

At home a bed is a good place to take time out for ideas. We might well devote a half-hour each week pondering creatively our family problems. Set aside a definite period, say on a Sunday afternoon. Go to your room, close the door, kick off your shoes, lie down. Pick yourself a creative chore.

In such ways we can go to bed, not to nap, but to awaken our imaginations. But, bed is also a good place for creative thinking even when we go to bed to try to sleep or to get well. One use of sleep is to let ideas simmer. By sleeping on ideas we often hatch out better ones. This can be far more productive if, before we turn out the lights, we actually jot down the best thoughts we have been able to dream up while awake. The very making of these notes tends to free our minds and thus enable us to fall asleep sooner. But those notes also tend to engrave our minds with thoughts on which our subconscious can work better while we sleep.

"The bed, the bedside pad and pencil," said Mr. Walter E. Irving, the inventor of emergency landing field mats for the Army, "are great aids to ideas and schemes." Another who believes that bed can be a hothouse for ideas is Alfred Hull. The creator of more new types of electron tubes than any other inventor, Hull has said that most of his best ideas have crept up on him "in the middle of the night."

Insomnia is a vicious circle. If we could realize that the usual reason we cannot sleep is that we do not need sleep, we could turn insomnia into an opportunity. We can pick on something for which we want ideas, and then roam our minds around that hunting ground. It can be fun. It may be profitable. It may bring sleep.

Next to the bedroom there is a tiled tower called the bathroom where our creative minds like to work. A good long shower or a hot tub often induce ideas. Shaving, like bathing, provides the same solitude, the same soothing sound of running water, and the same sense of well being. Still another reason why shaving and creative thinking can go together is that the mind is usually more creative in the early hours. "The muses love the morning," said Erasmus.

The exercise that seems to go best with creativity is just plain walking. I asked an M.I.T. graduate, "Who was the most creative of all your professors?" He said Dr. Warren K. Lewis. I asked if he knew whether Dr. Lewis consciously did things to make himself more creative. "I don't really know," said my cautious friend, "but he is a great one for hiking through the woods. It is common belief that he does this partly for exercise, but mainly as a help to his creative thinking." A walk through busy marts may likewise help.

Chores are good coaxers of creativity. While at work on a creative quest, an atmosphere of reverie may intensify the creative flame. Others claim that attending concerts kindles their creativity. Some think the ideal ivory tower is the stern of a boat. Something about a plane's whir and a train's rhythm tends to make creative juice flow.

My best idea was born on the subway. For months I had tried to think up a plan to mutualize the ownership of our company. One night I dined uptown at my brother's home. On the way back to the subway, I was about to buy a paper when it occurred to me that I might use those 20 minutes to get nearer to the idea. I found a seat and began to make notes. Pretty soon the car was crowded. The chatter was babel, and the noise of the train was bedlam. In the midst of all that I hit on the idea for which I had strained for so long. I wouldn't have landed it then if I had bought a newspaper or if I had forgotten my pencil.

With proper concentration it is possible to track down ideas anywhere, at any time. Concentration is nothing but attention, sharply focused and steadily sustained. It is an acquired habit rather than a native gift.

A good way to court concentration is to rub pencil against paper. For pads and pencils are keys to the kind of concentration which enables us to think, with or without an ivory tower.

IMAGINATION TAKES MANY FORMS, INCLUDING NON-CREATIVE

"What do you mean by imagination?" is a question I was asked after speaking at a banquet. The thesaurus lists over 50 synonyms. But, since all of us have imagination, each of us has a first knowledge of what it is and does. According to Gilbert Chesterton, English author and critic, none of us should belittle such self-understanding. "We can understand astronomy only by being astronomers. But, we can understand a great deal of anthropology merely because we are human. We are that which we study." By the same token, it is your imagination which you now study.

The many forms of imagination fall into two broad classes. One consists essentially of the kinds which *run themselves* and sometimes run away with us. The other class is made up of the kinds we can run—which we can *drive*, if and when we will. The first group is the non-creative. The second is the creative.

The non-creative includes uncontrollable and unhealthy forms such as hallucinations, delusions of grandeur, persecution complexes, and similar maladies. A basic cause of such complexes is the desire to run away from difficulty—to *misuse* one's imagination as a way to flee from reality.

The non-creative class also includes forms that are normal and, except for dreams, are largely controllable. Day-dreaming is the most common use of non-creative imagination. It takes less than no effort. We merely let our imaginations join hands with our memories and run here and there and everywhere. Dr. Josephine Jackson warns that day-dreaming may become unhealthy when "instead of turning a telescope on the world of reality—as positive imagination does—the negative variety refuses to even look with the naked eye.

Worry is a non-creative form of imagination. And then there are the blues. Isn't it a fact that when we are in the dumps, it is because our imagination is putting us over the jumps—instead of riding "our imagination with a strong enough rein."

CREATIVE IMAGINATION IS MANIFOLD AND INTERACTING

"Just imagine!" When you hear people say that, what do they mean? Something that is truly creative? No. They are probably referring to forms which are *almost* creative, quite controllable, and generally enjoyable. Let's scan some of these before we tackle the truly creative.

First there is *visual imagery*, the power to see things in the "mind's eye." There are three forms of visual imagery. *Speculative imagery* allows us to "see" something we have never actually seen. *Reproductive imagination* enables us deliberately to bring pictures back into our minds. The third form of visual imagination, called *structural visualization*, is an ability to construct three-dimensional forms in the mind's eye from a flat blueprint.

All three visual forms of imagination—whether fairly photographic or almost mathematically exact—are highly controllable, as we all know from the way we can operate our own mental cameras at will.

A more nearly creative form serves as a *bridge* by which we can put ourselves into another's place. We use this *vicarious* imagination most of the time. Sympathy is one of its facets. Without vicarious imagination we could not "feel for others." The Golden Rule embodies the noblest use of vicarious imagination. To "do unto others," we have to imagine how *they* would like to be treated. A similar call for imagination marks every act of kindness, such as the selection of gifts. To a degree, this calls for *creativity*, since we seldom pick the right gift without creative *effort*.

That brings us within a short step of creativity, but let's first look at one way in which our Aladdin's lamp serves somewhat as a light. Let's call this form *anticipative imagination*. In its most passive phase it is the instinct which stops children from touching live coals. Carried to extreme, anticipative imagination can be more than passive—it can be so active as to border on the creative. A newspaper owner was running for mayor of his city. A few days before election the publisher wrote two alternative headlines and had them set. One headline announced his election. The other read: FRAUD AT THE POLLS.

The highest form of anticipative imagination is *creative expectancy*. "When we look forward to something we want to come true, and strongly believe that it will come true, we can often make it come true." It is a faculty which characterizes a champion, whether he be a Babe Ruth, a Henry Ward Beecher, or an Abraham Lincoln.

Now for *truly creative imagination*. Its functions are mainly two-fold. One is to *hunt*, the other to *change* what is found.

In its hunting function, our Aladdin's lamp can serve us as a searchlight with which we can find that which is not really new, but is new to us. Newton lighted up unknown but existent truths such as the law of gravity. This is discovery rather than invention. But, for invention or discovery, we should always swing our searchlight here, there and everywhere. The more alternatives we uncover, the more likely we are to find what we seek.—and this is often found in the obvious.

A pencil will make any such hunt more fruitful. If we jot down one alternative after another, the very jotting down steps up our creative power; and each alternative we list is likely to light up another alternative, as we will see later when we get into *association of ideas.*

The *hunting* function should not be too sharply set apart from the *changing* function. But let's look at this *changing* function by itself for a moment. Just as our Aladdin's Lamp can be used for *light*, so can it be used for heat. As a cooker, imagination can bring together those things or thoughts which are not new of themselves, but can be cooked up into that which is new. In this way, we can do more than *discover*—we can *invent*—we can produce ideas that never before existed.

Creative imagination has been called a *catalyst*; but this, too, misses the point. As used in chemistry, a catalyst speeds up or slows down, whereas acceleration or deceleration is not a vital part of the creative process. The oft-used term of *synthesis* is likewise inadequate. Even the act of bringing things together into new combinations may take more than synthesis alone. Often it calls for breaking up into separate parts and then regrouping them. Analysis, hunting, combining and otherwise changing—these are all parts of creative research. Scientific experimentation calls into play all of these activities and more.

At home, in the office or in the lab, our hunting power finds for us the things that are. Our changing power makes things over in one way or another. Together they become the power that enables a creative thinker to arrive at new ideas.

Unlike other forms of imagination, creativity is seldom automatic. Even when it seems to work without bidding, it is usually because we have been *trying* to make it work. *Thus creativity is more than mere imagination. It is imagination inseparably coupled with both intent and effort.* Our Aladdin's lamp must not only be pointed but rubbed.

Physiologist R. W. Gerard described creative imagination as the "action of the mind which produces a new idea or insight." The key word in that statement is *action*. And when Joseph Jastrow termed creative effort "the imagination that looks forward, foresees, supplies, completes, plans, invents, solves, advances, originates," it is significant that there is not a single passive verb in his whole list.

THE CREATIVE FUEL WE STORE; IS IT RICH OR THIN?

"Many a man fails to become a good thinker for the sole reason that his *memory* is too good." When Friedrich Wilhelm Nietzsche wrote that, did he mean memory as mental *storage*—or as an ability to recall figures, facts, and names? If he meant the latter, Nietzsche may have been right. Mnemonics wastes mental energy that could go into creative thinking.

An over-active power of recall may even block creative thinking. When too prone to bring back the past, we tend to work our minds in the wrong direction. Creativity calls for forward thinking. Although creative imagination uses the materials of previous experience, the chief aim is not to reproduce the past—on the contrary, it is to avoid reproducing the past.

Nietzsche was wrong in decrying memory if, by memory, he meant our mental storehouse. A well-furnished mind is a vital part of creative power. Professor Charles Grandgent of Harvard wrote: "Imagination, like reason, cannot run without the gasoline of knowledge." And H. G. Schnackel said, "Any *addition* to the individual's store of usable experience is potential material for the exercise of the imagination."

First-hand experience provides the richest fuel for creative power. Second-hand experience—such as superficial reading, listening, or spectating—gives us far thinner fuel.

Having been born and brought up in the Bronx, I can't claim to be a country boy. But first-hand observation has convinced me that those raised on farms gain richer material for creative use than those reared in the city. This should be true, for surely we gain more from milking cows than seeing milkbottles on windowsills. Children who were running errands, working in stores and harvesting on neighboring farms, mentally stored first-hand material with which later to enrich their judgment and their creative power.

Edna Ferber laid great stress on creative gold gathered in youth. "I just took my childhood memories out the back of my head where they had been neatly stored for so many years and pinned them down on paper."

Think of the first-hand experience Thomas Alva Edison put under his belt at the age of twelve as candy-butcher on Grand Trunk trains. Think of the creative fuel he must have stored by publishing a newspaper when still under fourteen. Between times, he bought and sold fruit and vegetables, and, while still in his teens, he dashed-and-dotted in a telegraph office. So much did he learn first-hand that, by the time he was 22, he had perfected the Universal Stock Ticker and had sold it to Western Union for $40,000.

Hardship can force city children to gain riches by way of first-hand experience. Around the Bowery, another young man profited by hardship. This was Irving Berlin, whose four sisters did needlework in sweatshops, whose father scraped up his few dollars by chanting in synagogues and inspecting meat to make sure it was Kosher. As a singing waiter, Berlin grew rich in first-hand experience which he later recognized as a creative asset. "You can't write a song out of thin air, you have to know and feel what you are writing about."

Travel is another rich source. Eugene O'Neill combined travel with adversity. He became an office-secretary in New York, a gold-hunter in the Honduras jungle, a seaman on a Scandinavian windjammer, a sewing-machine repairman in Buenos Aires, a hide-sorter in La Plata, a loafer on the New York waterfront, a patient in a tuberculosis sanitarium. Thus, before his first play was published when he was 24, he had stored up the first-hand experience of a dozen lives.

Another source is reading. Taking in the movies, watching sports, listening to the radio—these are second-hand experiences which provide fuel far less rich than that stored by reading. As readers we put in at least a little effort. As supine spectators or idle listeners we put in none. For that reason, what we thus take in is too dilute.

Contacts are likely to be richer sources; but the richness depends on how we conduct our conversations. Ask fruitful questions. Be non-subjective. Listen hard. That sort of self-education certainly steps up creative power.

Alexander Graham Bell laid down a *Rule of Three* for self-education: (1) *Observe* as many worthwhile facts as possible, (2) *Remember* what has been observed, (3) *Compare* the facts so as to come to conclusions. "The wonderful thing about it," said Dr. Bell, "is that gaining an education in this way is not a penance, but a delight."

Some build standby tanks by way of special files, and fill them with creator fuel. Charlie Upson, head of the Upson Company at Lockport, has pioneered many new developments in fiberboard. Among his treasures are file upon file of references to countless ideas created by Ben Franklin.

THE POWER OF ASSOCIATION JOINS
MEMORY WITH IMAGINATION

"That reminds me." These three words sum up most of what is known about that part of our creative power called *association of ideas*—a faculty which gears imagination to memory. Association works harder for those whose imaginative talent is more intense and whose mental storage is lusher. In the main, it works automatically but can be sped up by effort.

The ancient Greeks laid down as the three laws of association: contiguity, similarity, and contrast. By contiguity they meant nearness, as when a baby's shoe reminds you of an infant. By similarity they merely meant that a picture of a lion will remind you of a cat. By contrast they meant that a midget might remind you of a giant. In the next 19 centuries, only one other law was added. This was Hume's law of "cause and effect," which meant that a yawn may remind you that it's time to retire.

Association can work in many ways. Figures of speech provide a parallel. Similarity, of course, is the prime law of association and a simile is the simplest of the figures based on similarity. The metaphor *implies* similarity. Association likewise works through sounds rather than words. Even smells invoke chains of thoughts.

Many students of imagination have stressed *combination* as the essence of creativity. "A creative thinker," said Dr. William Easton, "evolves no new ideas. He actually evolves new combinations of ideas that are already in his mind." Chain-thinking naturally contributes much to the creation of combinations. For most combinations are based on groupings of like things and thoughts; and similarity is the basic law of association.

The power of association can also lead us into creative undertakings. Wilbur and Orville Wright were wild about flying kites. They were in the bicycle business and had no thought of airplanes. One day they read about a German meeting his death in an attempt to glide off a mountain with giant wings fastened to his arms and a tail fastened to his back. That led the Wright brothers to construct a glider with nothing but sport in mind. One thing led to another, and history made by the Wrights at Kitty Hawk was directly due to that chain of ideas.

Especially when thinking creatively in groups, association is a powerful factor. We bat ideas around the table and one idea bumps into another existence. I say, "How about this—?" The person next to me listens and suddenly exclaims, "That gives me an idea!" Then that person sets forth a suggestion based on my first thought. And so it goes, one idea suggesting another and still another.

Daymond Aiken maintained that our power of association will produce more ideas if we keep a notebook and jot down our hunches, our observations, and our conclusions. "Ideas are flighty things," said Aiken.

The use of checklists can help make chain-linking yield more creative dividends. Clement Kieffer operates a strange kind of check-list in the form of a grab-bag. In charge of window displays for Kleinhan's store in Buffalo, he has won more prizes for his ideas than anyone in his line.

For his checklist he uses a big box into which he throws clippings and pieces of paper with notes or sketches of ideas he has thought up. His grab-bag bulges with over 3,000 such idea-starters. I asked him why he did not organize them in orderly files. "If I did that," he replied, "I would then go to just one place and pick up only one or two thoughts. I have found from experience that by pawing through hundreds of random ideas, I not only am more likely to get one that seems to fit my need—but, far more than that, I find that one idea suggests another, and after doing a lot of pawing, am apt to come up with something new and different from any in my grab-bag.'

Yes, grab-bags, checklists, note-pads, purposiveness, stick-to-it-iveness—with these we can cause our power of association to well up more ideas for us out of the storage-tanks called memory.

EMOTIONAL DRIVE AS A SOURCE OF CREATIVE POWER

In the main, the action of association is like momentum and is usually a bi-product of the energy we generate to empower our imagination. This force stems from two sources—our *emotions* and our *will*. Nearly all driving-power is a mixture of both.

Emotional drive is self-starting and largely automatic, whether based on hunger, fear, love or ambition. According to Dr. William Easton, even scientists must be motivated by "enthusiasm, devotions, passions, for creative thinking is not a purely intellectual process: on the contrary, the thinker is dominated by emotions from the start to the finish of their work."

We have always known that ideas flow faster under emotional stress. This does not mean that a crisis makes our creative talent any greater; it merely means that exigency can throw our emotional drive into high gear. Passion often works imagination too wildly in a life and death dilemma. Normally it is good creative policy to make our imagination shoot wild—as long as we have time later to choose our good ideas from our bad. But when a passion of panic overruns us, our imagination is too prone to go haywire. Fright is a treacherous drive.

Fear of punishment may make us work hard physically, but how can we focus our creative minds when obsessed by fear of punishment? Even the slightest degree of coercion tends to cramp imagination.

Dr. Howard E. Fritz, research head of the B.F. Goodrich Company, has pointed this out. "To induce creative thinking," he said, "we cannot dominate or threaten. Such methods will not and cannot inspire."

After the last war, our government sent to Germany my friend, Dr. Max E. Bretschger, one of America's most creative chemists. His mission was to determine how far German scientists might have gone ahead of us in creation of new chemicals for advanced warfare. German chemists had always been great chemists. Wouldn't you think that, under the Nazi whip, they would have been driven far beyond what our chemists had achieved?

"No," said Dr. Bretschger. "To our surprise we found that we had out-thought them." Because they were so concerned about their personal lives in the hands of Hitler, they could not drive their minds to get the most out of their imaginations.

Love is a steadier and better driving-power. Love of country inspired hundreds of thousands of our people to think up ideas that helped win the war.

"I address myself only to those among you who have ambition to become millionaires," Andrew Carnegie thus greeted a student-body. Gold does provide an emotional drive in pursuits including the creative. But the fear of poverty is even a stronger urge than the hope of riches. I know in my own case, my chronic drive goes back to a childhood of insecurity. As F. Wayland Vaughan pointed out, "Creative effort in times of prosperity has tended to ebb, whereas depressions have brought extra efforts that have resulted in many of the advancements which have put America ahead of the rest of the world."

The drive we need to make the most of our imagination is usually a mixture of inner urges and self-imposed spurts. But the habit of effort is the surest standby.

Very few will admit it, but just plain fun ultimately becomes one of the urges after a habit of creative effort has been formed. Even those who have to rub their lamps for a living often rub them for diversion. The editor of a great magazine, with two hours to spend on a train, amused himself by imagining himself to be a struggling publisher on a one-person weekly newspaper. Before he had reached his destination, he had thought up about 50 things he would do if his circulation were in the hundreds instead of the millions.

And so we run the gamut of emotional drives. With some, these are far more than with others. But, in the long run, our feelings are too unsteady as forces on which any of us can wholly rely for our creative power. We still have to do a lot of tugging on our bootstraps.

WHERE THERE'S A WILL THERE ARE WAYS TO THINK UP

Most of us agree that the average person must and can try hard to make imagination work; but a few still seem to feel that a genius just gushes ideas. The geniuses themselves say otherwise. Ideas have not come easily even to one as accomplished as E.M. Statler, who founded Statler Hotels. His personal secretary told me: "Although the hotel world thought of E.M. as a genius, I know that every one of his great ideas came from sweating and sweating hard."

We are no Pasteurs. So again comes the question as to whether average persons are up to such captaining of their minds. In answer, William James wrote, "The normal opener of deeper and deeper levels of energy is the will." And Brooks Atkinson attested: "Everyone can achieve a great deal . . . according to the burning intensity of their will and the keenness of the imagination."

Many young people have come to me for creative jobs and I have been amazed to find how few have ever called on their wills to work their imaginations. One of my test questions has been, "What did you ever try to think up on your own accord?" In nine out of ten cases the answer has been, "Nothing." How can they hope for creative responsibility when they have never learned the first lesson?

Some *hows* may help. One way to "put your mind to it" is to make a date with yourself—set a time and place. Most writers use this device. I asked Clarence Budington Kelland how he went to it. He confessed that he never would turn out a thing if he did not schedule himself—that each morning after breakfast he had to gird himself to start tapping his typewriter, and had to force himself to keep pounding hour after hour. He admitted that his genius is about 30 percent knack and 70 percent sweat.

Pick a place. As a rule, offices are less good for creative thinking than for judicial functioning. One man

I know has found he can ponder creative problems far better by staying at home. Once when I faced a hard creative task, I went to an inn over 100 miles away. Not only was I uninterrupted—not only did I get away from routine—but, because I had made such effort to go so far solely to engage in creative effort, my imagination seemed to work far better. The very taking of that trip tended to sharpen my imagination.

Set a deadline. Promise that you will have a certain number of ideas to offer at such-and-such a time. When you fix a deadline, you add emotional power lest you may fall down. Many creative people are driven by automatic deadlines. A columnist faces one each day. A minister's weekly deadline badgers him into creative action. Deadlines thrust upon us in business are often the spurs which win our spurs for us.

Team up. Make a date with somebody else.

To move the will into imaginative action, *pencils* can serve as crowbars. Although it's almost axiomatic that the more notes we make, the more ideas we are likely to produce, how few of us take advantage of this device. One week I went through six conferences in which about 100 people took part. Only three of them put down any notes.

Note-taking helps in several ways. It empowers association, it piles up alternatives, it stores rich fuel that otherwise would trickle out through our forgettery. But, above all, note-taking of itself induces a spirit of effort.

When the George Batten Company merged with Barton, Durstine and Osborn, William H. Johns of the George Batten Company became Chairman of the Board. Mr. Johns' secret weapons were pencils. He went to great lengths to choose them, importing some from Germany; having others made solely for him by the American Pencil Company. Then, finding the usual memo-book and 3 × 5 cards too cumbersome to use, he designed a form 8" long and only 2½" wide, made of cardboard stiff enough to stand up and almost stick out of his inside pocket. Several of us adopted the note-cards and, for further "come-on," we had these red-letter words printed on the top of each side: "For Notes and *Ideas*."

A good way to get going is to give yourself a quota. Suppose you first set for yourself a stint of only five ideas. To think up those five, others will occur; and the first thing you know you will be on your way to 25. And the more ideas, the more likely it will be that one of them will hit the bull's-eye. It is best to make your aim specific.

Creativity also calls for *keeping going*. We too often give up too easily and too early, mainly because we tend to over-rate the power of inspiration and wait for lightning to strike us. Why don't we realize that the way to start is to start, and that there is no truth stronger than the old maxim of "try and try again?" The renowned rowing coach Ten Eyck used to nag his crews with this: "If you hang on two strokes longer than your opponents, you will lick 'em." That would be a good motto to put on the desk of anyone who wants to pull ahead in the creative race.

As Abraham Lincoln said: "When I got on a hunt for an idea, I could not sleep until I had caught it." And yet can't all of us—by keeping our imaginations on the grindstone just a little longer—spark more ideas and step up our creative power?

JUDGMENT MAY CHOKE IDEAS; LET'S KEEP IT IN ITS PLACE

"Good judgment is the test of a trained mind." So said Matthew Thompson McClure, who thus joined John Dewey and other thinkers in putting the judicial mind on a pedestal. But in a creative effort, judgment is good only when *properly trained.*

Judicial effort and creative effort are alike in that both call for analysis and synthesis. The judicial mind breaks facts down, weighs them, compares them, rejects some, keeps other—and then puts together the resultant elements to form a conclusion. The creative mind does much the same, except that the end-product is an idea instead of a verdict. Then, too, whereas judgment tends to confine itself to facts in hand, imagination has to reach out for the unknown—almost to the point of making two and two something more important than four.

Of course judgment is important. But if we had had nothing but a judicial faculty where would we be? Without imagination the world would probably still be in a primitive state—with everything so simple, so judged and re-judged over the centuries, that even judgment would be unimportant.

Compared to creative effort, judicial effort is far easier. Pros ands cons "come" to us without strain. Even analysis is relatively easy.

Basically there are two kinds of judgment—critical judgment and constructive judgment. The critical calls mainly for knowledge, whereas the constructive may need help from imagination. Is nylon better than silk? This calls for a simple process of critical analysis. "Should we do this or that?" Here we have to think up all possible alternatives, and foresee results. We have to ask ourselves questions such as, "What are the consequences?" "What if others did that?" "What if conditions change?" And in each case we have to tap imagination for the answer.

In the average person, judgment grows automatically with years, while creativity dwindles unless consciously kept up. Circumstances force us to use our judicial mind every waking hour. And by exercise it grows, or should grow, better and stronger.

Then, too, education makes our judgment grow. We study mathematics, we study logic, we learn to debate, we read history, we discuss pros and cons. Over 90 percent of our education tends to train and strengthen our judicial faculties. Still another influence tends to do the same—it's stylish to be an unerring judge. "How wonderful—he never makes any mistakes." You hear that 10 times as often as you hear, "She has imagination—and makes it work."

We are so quick to offer our opinion; and it is this tendency to criticize too soon that makes judgment so great a threat to creative effort. A good slogan for all of us would be, "Judge wisely but at the right time."

The fact that moods won't mix largely explains why the judicial and the creative tend to clash. Unless properly coordinated, each may mar the working of the other. The right mood for judicial thinking is largely negative. "What's wrong with this?" "Are we sure this won't be a mistake?"

In contrast, our creative thinking calls for a positive attitude. We have to be hopeful. We need enthusiasm. We have to encourage ourselves to the point of self-confidence. We have to beware of perfectionism lest it be abortive. Edison's first lamp was a crude affair. He must have realized that—must have known that it would certainly be improved—if not by him, by somebody else. He could have hung onto his imperfect model while he tried and tried to make it better. Or he could have junked the whole idea. He didn't do either. His first electric lamps were better than candles, kerosene lamps, or gaslights—so he introduced them. Then he went to work on improvements.

Dr. Suits of G.E. has declared the positive attitude "a characteristic of creative people." He urges: "Form the habit of reacting *Yes* to a new idea. First think of all the reasons why it's good. There will be plenty of people around to tell you why it won't work." Premature judgment may douse our creative flames, and even wash away ideas already generated.

Creative success is usually in ratio to the number of alternatives thought up. Thus, if we conceive 100 alternatives, our chances of landing the right idea are more than 10 times greater than if we stop 10 alternatives.

We might even make a conscious effort to think up the wildest ideas that could possibly apply. For at this point, we are just warming up our think-up apparatus—limbering up our imaginative muscles. Instead of laughing at such preliminary flashes—fantastic as they might seem to Old Man Judgment—we should put them down on paper. One of them might turn out to be as sensible as a doorkey.

Of the ways to prevent judgment from cramping creativeness, we have already touched on the main method; and this is to delay judgment—not only suspend it, but postpone it until our ingenuity has piled up all possible ideas. Even at that point we first let our minds coast awhile. Mental loafing at the right time induces inspiration, which may either add other ideas—or may combine into a better idea two or more of the many we have already thought up.

When it comes to judging, if we can test, rather than opine, so much the better. When ideas, instead of being tested, are subjected to personal judgment, a powerful debater can kill the better ones and enable the less fit to survive. Not only that—but, in the very process of testing ideas, new ideas are more likely to crop up, or at least, to stand up.

Let's not let the judgment throttle imagination. Let's not allow our critic to sap our creative energy.

LET'S NOT TRY TO UNDERMINE OUR OWN CREATIVE POWER

Long experience as a creative coach has opened my eyes to the way so many of us *undermine* our own creative power. Creative effort will always breed discouragement by *others* as long as nearly everyone likes to throw cold water. But *self*-discouragement—what a stifler of creativity this so often is, and how uncalled for! We should remember that even the Edisons fumbled and stumbled. And we should bear in mind that we are not aiming to become Edisons, but merely to step up our creative power somewhat—just enough to brighten our lives and help us get ahead. To do even that, we need some degree of self-encouragement.

Many young people lack the courage to advance an idea. This has led to a fallacy that one can get ahead in a job by "keeping one's nose clean"—and faster than by spouting ideas. As a result, the mortality of good ideas in infancy is appalling. And most of them are strangled by their own parents before anyone ever hears about them.

A tendency that militates against our creativity is our yen to conform. This carries the curse of conventionalism and convention is a great discourager of originality. To be more creative, we have to take ourselves by the scruff of the neck and warn ourselves against being copy-cats. "For fear I'll look foolish" goes with wanting not to seem different. This fear has stood in the way of many. I have tried to point out that truly intelligent people secretly admire creative effort, realizing as they do that almost all the good in the world came from somebody's "foolish" ideas.

Timidity is the arch gremlin. When due to our expecting too much of ourselves, diffidence may reflect conceit rather than modesty. One night, a group of us went into a huddle to think up a new radio show. All of us oldsters came through with ideas; but the youngsters just listened. I knew one of them to be gifted with far more creative talent than I, so I asked him: "Why didn't you do some pitching?" He explained to *his* satisfaction, but not to mine: "I was afraid you might not think my ideas were as good as you'd expect of me." He held back, not because he felt he was creatively sterile, but because he prided himself too much.

On the other hand, I have found that timidity usually stems from genuine doubts of one's ability to be creative. Such "doubts are traitors," quoth Shakespeare, "and make us lose the good we might oft win by fearing the attempt." Surely there can be no reasonable doubt that we do have imaginative talent, or that we can use it better if we will.

But even when we do think up, we are too often held back by hesitation to give out. Dr. Norman Peale said: "The trouble is that we do not sufficiently trust ourselves to create and deliver ideas." Carl Holmes was right when he remarked, "The more creative thinking we do, and the more ideas we give out, the more competent we become, and with this comes a satisfying sense of accomplishment."

Timidity also tends to halt us after we get started. A friend of mine had come up with the idea of sand-blasting a small area on glass canning jars so that labels would adhere better. He was so enthusiastic about his idea that he put up the money for a patent search, only to find that his idea had been patented in 1882. I was afraid that might slow up his creative effort, but no. "Of course it was a disappointment," he said, "but I realize that any would-be thinker-upper is sure to run into dead ends, just as he's sure, now and then, to stumble on something good if he makes enough tries."

In getting going, keeping going, or giving out, we have every reason to sweep timidity aside and gird our efforts with courage. More than that, we will do best to carry that courage to the point of audacity, and here's why: In creative activity, the wilder we shoot, the more and bigger ideas we are likely to be. Let's not forget that almost all good ideas are crazy at birth. Can you beat it?—they are going to put out a refrigerator which freezes ice with a gas-flame! What!—a ventriloquist on the radio! Yes, let's not only have the courage of our ideas, but let's risk the wild. There will always be plenty of people to tame them.

TWO

Preparation for Creativity

OTHERS CAN HELP MAKE OR MAR OUR CREATIVITY

Granted that historian Thomas Carlyle was right in saying, "a certain amount of opposition is a great help," creativity is so delicate a flower that praise tends to make it bloom while discouragement often nips it in the bud. Any of us will put out more and better ideas if our efforts are appreciated. Unfriendliness can make us stop trying. Wisecracks can be poison—as brought out by Balzac's epigram, "Paris is a city where great ideas perish, done to death by witticism." Every idea should elicit receptivity if not praise. Even if no good, it should at least call for encouragement to keep trying.

A boss is at their best when both a suggestor of ideas and a creative coach. I had many a talk with E.M. Statler. Mt. Statler didn't pride himself so much on his own ideas as on his ability to coax ideas out of others. "When I was a bellboy at the McClure House in Wheeling, I had to run up and down stairs toting pitchers of water. That's what led me to the idea of piping ice-water to each guestroom. Now that I am running my own hotels, I never fail to realize that someone who works in my hotels could dish up just as good an idea."

E.M. Statler had come up from the bottom and was the owner. It is much harder to induce such an attitude in supervisory employees. Whenever a management can lead supervisors to act as creative coaches, a happier and harder-hitting organization is sure to result. Ideas are generated best in an atmosphere of friendliness. No stimulus to creative effort is as effective as a good pat on the back.

What should an employee's attitude be toward ideas? *The best policy is always to keep suggesting. You may develop a reputation as a crackpot, but as soon as one or two of your ideas materialize your employer and co-workers begin to give you serious consideration.*

The greatest lesson an employee must learn is not to take rebuffs personally. Also, don't be too insistent. At times your employer may not seem receptive to your suggestions. Try again at a later time. Tell them you've been thinking it over and have some further evidence that your idea may be sound.

At all levels in an organization, the main cause is that old devil pride—pride in *judgment*. A sense of judicial superiority forces many of us to greet our fellow-worker's idea with a sneer.

The discouragement that hurts the most is that which comes from those we love. Most of us start life with lots of imagination and yet many of us grow up to be men and women with not an idea in our heads. Why? As a nation we have not made enough of the *importance* of ideas, and have not admitted that creative power *can be developed*. Another reason is that oldsters so deliberately discourage youngsters. The fact is that nearly all of us are guilty of active discouragement, or at least, of lack of creative encouragement.

Dr. Roma Gans has stressed the need to build self-confidence in the young. Dr. Gans urged that the child be given a chance to feel smarter than grown-ups—that any time a child performed some stunt and demanded, "Can you do that?" we should say, "No, I can't. What's more, I never could." Dr. Gans further points out that there's a difference between a child's willingness to try *three* things—getting two successes and one flop—and trying only *one* thing that can be perfectly done. In her opinion the perfectionist point of view makes for narrowness of living, and of course, it can't help but cramp creative effort.

Brothers and sisters tend to look for a laugh in anything the other has done or tried to do. It may be too much to hope that brothers and sisters will encourage each other in creative sallies, but how much less harm would they do if they resisted the temptation to discourage. Uncles, aunts, and grandparents are less cruel in this respect. As a rule they instinctively tend to enhearten rather than dishearten.

Discouragement by outsiders is easier to take than that which comes from associates or relatives, but still we have to steel ourselves against even that. One way to gird our wills is to realize that most of the greatest ideas were at first greeted with sneers. When Charles Newbold worked out the idea of a cast-iron plow, the farmers rejected it on the grounds that iron polluted the soil and encouraged weeds. In 1844, Dr. Horace

Wells was the first to use gas on patients while pulling teeth. The medical profession squelched this new idea as a humbug.

Let's remember that we can throttle our own creative talent by self-discouragement. Let's also remember that we can throttle the creative talent in others in the same way. *For all of us, a good rule is always to encourage ideas—to encourage speaking up as well as thinking up.*

EVEN EXERCISE CAN BE FUN, ESPECIALLY IN CREATIVE THINKING

"Jumping to Conclusions" is the only exercise some minds get, and that's not even thinking; for to think is "to exercise the mind otherwise than by passive reception of another's ideas." So says the Oxford Dictionary, and thinking—especially *creative* thinking—*is exercise*. "You must use it or you lose it," a favorite expression of Bishop Norman Nash of Massachusetts, applies strongly to one's creative talent.

Reading packs the memory and thus enriches our power of association. As a creative exercise, it falls short in that it takes so little effort. It depends on how much energy we put into our reading and what we read. Certain periodicals are rich with material that stimulates imagination. Biographies, through inspiration, can likewise help our creative power. Certain books on thinking can make us better able to understand our minds, and through such understanding enable us to make more intelligent use of our creative gift. Of all fiction, the mystery books seem to offer the most exercise to our creative muscles—especially if we read them with an attitude of participation rather than spectatorship.

Games can be good exercise as well as fun. In chess, for example, the players have to think forward—are forced to pile up many alternatives before choosing the right one. And chess also induces mental sweat.

Among parlor games, "Twenty Questions" gives no creative exercise to those merely answering yes or no, although the questioner does have to run their mind around energetically in search of alternatives. A far better game is charades. This provides creative exercise for all participants.

Particularly in colleges there is a need for games in which young people can use their idea-machinery.

An editor recently said: "Students spend too much of their time taking in and too little giving out. Why not an 'Idea' Club?"

Quizzes and puzzles can likewise be creative exercises. Thomas Edison was a believer in these. According to his son Charles, Edison originated the first quizzes which became the forerunners of the crossword puzzle.

Actual doing is, of course, the best exercise. The way to create is to create, just the way to write is to write. Some of us believe Winston Churchill to be not only the greatest figure but also the greatest creative mind of our time. The things he thought up to keep England out of Hitler's grasp are a lasting tribute to man's power of imagination. To a large extent it was his training in writing that made him stand out creatively. While his fellow-officers loafed through their Army days in India and other hot countries, Churchill wrote and wrote and wrote.

Others have simpler ways to exercise their mental muscles. A college president told me about his "daily dozen." Busy as he is, he makes himself think up one brand new simile each day. The night he told me this, I asked him what was the one he had thought up that day. Promptly he replied, "As chaste as the kiss of billiard balls."

A young lawyer recently won a spectacular victory. When I asked a newspaper reporter about this, he said: "Based on knowledge of law, that young man could never have won the case. It was his ingenuity that turned the trick—his ability to think up new ways to prove to the jury that his client was right and his opponent's client was wrong! His mental practice consists of thinking up stories for children, night after night, year after year. His improvised tales may not be as good as the printed ones, but his children like them even better."

Of course when you keep on creating, even trivially, you tend to form a habit. Getting started soon becomes less of a problem. The more you try, the more you instinctively do as Victor Wagner urged, when he said: "Ask questions, dig for facts, gather experience, watch the breaks. And at every stage of the game, peer beyond the end of your nose, learn that two and two can make 22 and zero as well as four—and above all get your gift of imagination to work." Once that trick becomes a habit, as it always does, you will realize as the thousands who did it before, that imagination, like faith, can and often does move mountains.

TO ATTACK A CREATIVE TASK
WE FIRST GET SET

Now we come to how to tackle a creative project. The first step is to *get set*—to establish the "working mood" which all agree is vital to purposeful creativity. I have watched ad-writer Alan Ward day by day for 20 years. How does he go about flexing his mental muscles?

"I close my office door and try to limber up. I try to forget everything but the job before me. Then I pull my typewriter to me, wrap my legs around it, and start to write. I write down every line that comes into my head. Crazy, dull, however it sounds. I find that if I don't, it may linger there and block others. I write as fast as I can. And then, after a long while, some cogs that haven't worked start to whir, and something striking begins to tap itself out on the yellow sheet before me—like a telegraph message. That's the hard way and the only way I know on most days." Ward *helps himself* to be creative.

Albert Edward Wiggam, author and philosopher, has described the line between the "open-minders and tight-minders" as "sharp and clean-cut." He rightfully declared the open-minded to be "the only people who have ever contributed anything to human progress." But hardly any intelligent mind is chronically closed. Nearly all of us are more or less open-minded and can be completely so at times. A good time to help make oneself that way is when starting a creative task.

Even the open-minded may have to ward off influences that could close their minds while in quest of an idea. It would have been easy for Pasteur to have taken for granted the cause of silkworm disease when he went to the south of France to save it from ruin. The local silkworm-growers tried to tell him just what the disease was and what caused it. Had he heeded their theories, he might never have found the answer that meant so much to France.

Dr. Suits of General Electric lays great stress on being open-minded to one's hunches. "Be on the alert for hunches,' he urged, "and whenever you find one hovering on the threshold of your consciousness, welcome it with open arms. Doing these things won't transform you into a genius overnight. But they're guaranteed to help you locate the treasure chest of ideas which lies hidden at the back of your own brain."

The German psychologists made much of what they called "Aufgabe." As I get it, this means interest sharpened to the point of all-out intent. This frame of mind is certainly important to a creative undertaking. Intent is stronger when we have a goal. There is no easy escape for creative thinkers who have to work on assignments not of their own choosing. Industrial researchers, illustrators, those in advertising, and others in commercial lines, are often given tasks which do not interest them, and they therefore have to force themselves into enough intent to start creating. Whether self-generated or not, an intense interest is needed for any creative task, for otherwise, we cannot fully command the services of our imagination.

All-out intent begets all-around awareness, which also helps to get us to first base creatively. In my newspaper days, such awareness was known as a "nose for news" and is still the distinguishing mark of star reporters. But even chemists can set themselves apart by developing the same power. Through awareness we can multiply our intake of materials for our minds to sort out and to apply to specific creative problems. In essence a good idea is usually based on the particular problem we're attacking, plus general facts we have accumulated in our cerebral warehouse. For this reason alone, we should consciously keep our eyes and ears wide open.

When awareness goes beyond receptivity, it becomes active curiosity. This may or may not kill cats; but it is certain that the greater our curiosity, the more lives we can live creatively.

But, curiosity is not enough to insure enough awareness. Awareness at the best calls for conscious action. "Our creative urge," said Fryer and Henry, "has to be perpetually pricked and goaded and jogged into a wide-awake state of awareness. Get yourself into seeing things about you, feeling things. By virtue of your very 'awareness' your mind will start effervescing."

So before we set our aim, let's flex ourselves, open out minds, intensify our intent, court awareness, encourage curiosity and then tug that bootstrap marked "concentration." Thus we can get into a working mood where effort is more like a sport.

LET'S NOW PICK OUR TARGET
AND SET OUR AIM

Although, at times, an idea is accidentally stumbled upon, it usually turns out that the stumbler had been hard on its trail. A good aim is needed as a starter and as a means of focus. But first we must make our target clear. Often we must think up just what we are going to *try* to think up.

Dr. Charles M. A. Stine did not know what he was after when he started the search for nylon. At Du Pont his associates have told me that his outstanding point is curiosity. There would probably be no nylon had he not asked the question: "I wonder what would happen if molecules were rearranged so that they would be in lines instead of clusters?" Dr. Stine thus created a target which he then handed to Dr. Wallace Hume Carothers. As leader of the scientific team which first synthesized Du Pont nylon, Dr. Carothers was highly honored by his company. When he died in 1937, at the age of 41, the Nylon Research Laboratory was dedicated in his honor as the "Carothers Research Laboratory."

Would Dr. Carothers' name now be immortalized had it not been for Dr. Stine's originality in setting the target for him? Who deserves the greater credit—the instigator or the worker-out-er? Surely, the aim itself is often more than half the battle.

Let's make the target clear. "Specify your problem consciously," urged Brand Blanshard of Yale. By all means let's *write out* the problem and commit ourselves to find *an* answer, if not *the* answer.

Let's adopt Brand Blanshard's technique and convert our target into specific questions. Walter Chrysler saved his small pay as a young railroad mechanic in order to buy a huge $5,000 Pierce-Arrow. He wanted to find a way to make a better motorcar and went at it by asking himself specific questions such as "Why wouldn't brakes on all four wheels stop the car even better?" "Why not keep the lubricating oil in better condition by having it run through a filter all the while?" His first Chrysler automobile was the sensation of that year's auto show.

Just as one idea leads to another, one aim often leads to another. The Corning Glass people aimed to make globes for railroad lanterns so strong that they would not crack even when bombarded by icy sleet. They hit that mark all right and railroads became safer as a result. But in doing that, they perfected a new kind of glass—Pyrex.

It pays to assay our aims. The U.S. Patent Office is crowded with "good" ideas that are no good for anything. Therefore, before we set our aim, we might well stop and analyze. Let's select aims that mean something.

As has been pointed out, judicial judgment is often an enemy of creativity and should be kept in place. One of the times we should call in our judgment is right after we have tentatively picked a target. At this point, our judicial mind should tell us whether our target is worth shooting at.

Let's pick our target, and set our aim. And in narrowing our aim, let's not get the notion that all phases of creativity call for a sharp focus. For it is less important to *narrow* our aim than it is to *broaden* our search, after we get going.

BREAK DOWN THE PROBLEM;
FILL IN THE FACTS

Our memories can bring up almost enough knowledge for most of our creative sorties; but, when waging any major campaign for ideas, we have to augment our memories with new facts. To know what new facts are needed, we have to break down our problem.

Analysis of any kind can of itself bear creative fruit; for it tends to uncover clues which speed up our power of association and thus feed our imagination. And, in turn, imagination plays a guiding part in analysis. In fact, in *any* form of thinking, "imagination supplies the premises and asks the questions from which reason grinds out the conclusions as a calculating machine supplies answers." Dr. R. W. Gerard of the University of Chicago is the authority for that.

Questions are bone-and-sinew of analysis. "Why?" is almost always the main question, since cause-and-effect is usually the most important fact to find. So we have to delve into the *why-so* and *what-if.*

"The *first* step is always to set up the problem," said business leader and inventor Charles Kettering. In setting up procedure, sequence is often important. Of course, if we have a large enough staff, we can tackle all phases at once. Such was the case with the Manhattan Project—and likewise with the General Electric Company when called upon during the war to create a jet-plane almost overnight.

These steps will necessarily vary with circumstances; but in all cases, one of the first is to use the imagination to construct, out of the data supplied by memory and observation, a framework of ideas that will serve as a foundation for further work. A writer might prepare an outline; a scientist draws inferences to form a hypothesis. Without imagination, there would be no framework and the thinker would never get started on a project.

Charles Kettering has held that we can get too many facts at the wrong stages of our creative projects. John Livingston Lowes, professor and author, has strongly pointed out that "facts may swamp the imagination."

In one month I had to create two plans—one for an enlistment drive, another for a money-raising campaign. For the former plan my exhaustive study of comparable programs lulled me into a willingness to adapt, and thus shut me off from thinking up anything new. In preparing the other plan, I lined up the salient facts and then deliberately ignored what others had done. I found I could make my imagination work more radically. The resultant plan turned out to be far better than the other.

Such experiences indicate that, instead of doing an exhaustive job digging before starting to create, we might well line up a few fundamental facts and then start thinking up all the ideas we possibly can. After listing 50 or 100 such ideas, we could go back to our fact-finding.

There are two kinds of specific facts we should seek—those which are inherent in our problem and those which may have some bearing. Good prospecting calls for an open mind and for wide exposure; and our prospecting should dig deeper than mere sensing. We should delve into the how and the why. New facts as to cause are often all-important.

The need for new facts may be so far-reaching that it calls for a new and complete education, as illustrated in the story of Alexander Graham Bell. "As a young, unknown man," said Dr. Bell, "I went to Washington to talk with Professor Henry, an authority on electricity, about an idea I had conceived for transmitting speech by wires. He told me he thought I had the germ of a great invention. I told him, however, that I had not the electrical knowledge necessary to bring it into existence. He replied, '*Get it!*'" Dr. Bell had studied sound all his life. More than anyone, he knew the shapes of vibrations that pass through the air when we talk. But he had to—and did—absorb a new subject, electricity, in order to transform his notion into a telephone.

But again, it all depends. Charles Kettering has warned against leaning too much on textbooks. Another leading researcher told me he guards himself against their over-use when on a creative pursuit, and added, "For one thing, the facts in a textbook may be out of date. It takes a year to write such a book, a year to get it out, and the chances are it's at least three years old when you hunt for helpful facts in its pages."

In addition to finding new facts, we need to discover *relationships*. For instance, digging for *likenesses* can sometimes unearth a common factor which can serve as a *principle* in guiding our creative thinking. That's how Billy Rose got started on his career as a songwriter. Although he was the world's champion at shorthand, his heart was set on Tin Pin Alley. He realized how untutored he was for a music writing career, so he went into an orgy of preparatory analysis which Maurice Zolotow reported as follows: "Billy Rose repaired to the New York Public Library and each day, for many months, he studied the origins, history, leading exemplars, and techniques of American threnody.

He then toted up the salient characteristics of each, and estimated which group made the most money. The succession-of-sound songs—simple, repetitious, easy to memorize—were the songs most likely to become famous in the shortest span of time."

Thus Billy hit on the principle that had proved successful in songs like his *Barney Google with His Goo-Goo-Googly Eyes.* Within the next 10 years or so, he turned out nearly 400 popular songs.

Likenesses, yes, but differences, too, should be analyzed. In fact there are about a dozen such headings under which relationships can be built. The categories are largely sub-divisions of the three main laws of association. And logically so because the very process of relating facts and impressions is an almost automatic function of our power of association. Deliberate thinking-through tends to step up this power of ours.

As to the laws of association, let's first take contiguity—and this includes sequence as well as cause-and-effect. Let's ask these questions of any facts we have sought out: "This is *next* to what?" "What does this go with?" "What happens before or after?" "This is *smaller* than what, or *larger* than what?" "What would *cause* this effect?"

Similarity, the second law of association, covers likeness, sameness, composition and the common factor. Thus, under similarity we could relate our data by asking: "What is this *like*?" "What attribute has this in *common* with that?" Isn't this the *same* as that?" "What about the *component parts*?"

The third law of association is contrast, which includes difference as well as oppositeness. Thus we can relate our facts through queries such as: "What is this *unlike*?" "What is the point of *difference*?" "What about the *opposite*?" "How about *vice-versa*?"

And so it is that in a creative project, the final steps by way of preparation are these: (1) To break down our problem, (2) To build a framework, (3) To fill in the facts, (4) To relate our facts so as to give ourselves every chance of forming a *pattern*. For a pattern can become a magic map by which to reach the idea we pursue.

LET'S SEND FORTH OUR IMAGINATION IN SEARCH OF ALTERNATIVES

How can we give directions to our imagination? One good way is to ask ourselves questions. Why? Where?

When? Who? What? How? Truly creative thinking has to be guided by stabs such as, *"What about . . .?"* and *"What if . . .?"* And always it must be prodded with, *"What else?"* and again, *"What else?"*

It is a truism in golf that the lowest-scoring pros are not the best instructors. In most cases they acquired their swings as kids. In later years, their technique is so instinctive that they find it hard to tell pupils what they should consciously try to do to better their scores.

It's almost like that in creativity. The geniuses just don't know how they do it. A few even claim that there can be no techniques, and, rightly so, if technique means a rigid set of rules. Any attempt to lay down hard-and-fast methods would be naught but terminology masquerading as technology. But the genius is wrong to hold that there can be no *principles*, or "guides to procedure" as defined by Webster.

The basic principle is variation. The active adjunct to the principle of variation is plenty of alternatives. To pile these up, there are scores of directions for our imaginations to take. About 10 of these are highways, each of which leads to about 10 byways.

How does each principle of plentiful variation fit in with correlation and combination—these being the two principles most frequently laid down by authorities in the creative mind? The answer is that variation includes both and more. Almost every new idea is a combination of old ideas. But if we limit out creative effort strictly to the field of combination, we cannot help but limit our resultant alternatives and thus restrict our creativity.

And what about the principle of correlation? Relationships of things to things and thoughts to thoughts are decidedly inherent in all good creative thinking. Relationship is the basis of our power of association.

As a rule, the more often, the more freely we swing our imagination, the better—with the one reservation that we should never overlook the obvious. For the best answer to a creative problem is sometimes as plain as a planet.

It may pay to pay attention to the preposterous. Many a wild seed has reaped a harvest. Scientists use more wildness than we realize. Of Pasteur, Paul de Kruif said, "This man was a passionate groper whose head was incessantly inventing right theories and wrong guesses—shooting them out like a display of village fireworks going off bewilderingly by accident."

Of course, we should make a list of all our ideas. We can use this as a checklist to help us pile up more.

Always we should keep asking our imagination: "What else?" and again, "What else?"

We think of Irving Berlin as turning out one masterpiece after another. But the fact is that in between hits he made scores of mediocre stabs. He was a demon for quantity, according to Alexander Woollcott who said: "In his early days, he poured songs out so fast that his publishers thought it best to pretend that he was several persons." At least one song was launched under the name of Ren G. May. If you meditate on the letters of that implausible name you will see that they spell Germany, of which nation Berlin was the capital.

"Yes, but what about quality?" you might ask. Isn't it obvious that quantity breeds quality in creative effort? Not only are logic and mathematics on the side of the argument that the more ideas, the more likely that some of them may be good; but likewise it is true that the best ideas seldom come first. As Herbert Spencer said, "Early ideas are not usually true ideas."

My friend Welles Moot, among other things, is head of Sylvanite Mines. He tells me it takes four tons of ore to get one ounce of gold. Isn't creative mining like that with the more ore, by way of alternatives, yielding the more gold by way of gold ideas?

We might even call on our imaginations to help seduce ourselves into piling up enough alternatives. To that end, I thought up a trick to play on myself. Having found that the first alternatives come easily, I wanted an incentive to make me strive for the next and the next and the next. So I wrote out a table of prices, all imaginary of course. By this my first ideas would be worth one cent, my second worth two cents, my third worth four cents, my fourth eight cents, my fifth 16 cents—and so on, doubling the price for each additional alternative. Thus, when I have brainstorming to do and get 20 ideas written down on my list, I look at my table and see how much, on that basis, I would be paid for my 21st idea. Wow! It would be worth $10,485. For my 25th idea, my theoretical pay would be $167,772. This may sound childish, but it dramatizes to me the cold logic of the fact that the more alternatives I pile up, the more valuable my ideas are likely to be.

TO WHAT OTHER USES
COULD THIS BE PUT?

"To what other uses could *this* be put?" is a good question to ask of our imaginations in regard to a thing, a thought or a talent. For by adding uses we can often add values. Then, too, by piling up alternatives by way of uses, a *better* use is likely to come to light.

"In what other products could my material be used?" This is an obvious question to ask ourselves when we have a certain material and want to widen its market. Dr. George Washington Carver thought up over 300 useful articles in which peanuts could be used. For the home alone, he worked up over 105 different ways to prepare peanuts for the table.

I happened to be in on the start of fiberglass. Our big creative problem was, "To what uses could glass thread be put?" We dreamed up hundreds of applications; but hundreds more have since been thought up.

"To what use can waste be put?" Along this trail, the piling up of alternatives is particularly important. America's packing industry has been built on ingenuity in finding new uses for by-products—almost all by-products except the "pig's whistle."

The other-use trail need not be limited to things. When it comes to intangibles like principles, we might also ask our imagination, "To what use could this thought be put?"

Pure science becomes practical science by thinking up ways to use an academic discovery. Lord Lister thought Louis Pasteur was more or less guilty of boondoggling in trying to find a way to make wine stay sweet. But this work of Pasteur's led Lister to wonder whether a more important use could be found for Pasteur's findings. Specifically, he asked himself: "If germs ruin flavor, could germs be the cause of so many unexplained fatalities in surgery?" This other use of Pasteur's new theory led to proof that germs did invade wounds and this truth became the key to antiseptic surgery which immortalized Lister's name.

Piling up alternatives by way of new uses can do much to make the most of talents. Imagination can help a lot in vocational guidance. Four young artists who found their landscapes not quite good enough to sell decided to think up different ways in which they could use their skills. One became a well-paid painter of pictures on drums used in bands. Another specializes in clay models for museums. The third does well by painting faces on "character" dolls. The fourth now paints portraits of dogs, cats, and horses for their proud owners.

"What *new* use?" "What *other* use?" All of us have enough creative power to pile up alternatives galore by sending our imaginations along this highway and into its many byways.

WHAT CAN WE BORROW AND ADAPT TO OUR NEED?

"What is there *like* this, from which I might get an idea?" "Is there something *similar* I could partially copy?"

Ah—but how about plagiarism and infringement? True, it is legally and morally wrong to steal outright from someone, especially if by so doing we do harm. But just to take a lead from what someone else has thought up—this is a legitimate practice.

More often the adaptation is but partial. Baseball, for instance, was adapted from the English sport of "rounders." Football came from rugby. Basketball is about the only game originated in America.

It is well-nigh impossible for writers not to adapt. Goethe claimed there were only 36 basic plots. Willa Cather said, "There are only two or three human stories, and they go on repeating themselves as fiercely as if they had never happened before."

As to humor, George Lewis of the Gag Writers Institute claimed that in every "new" joke he could detect the skeleton of one of six gags.

In music many well-known hits have been re-births of classics. One example is *Till the End of Time*. This was taken from Chopin's *Polonaise*. *Andantino in D Flat* was the source of *Moonlight and Roses*.

New York's Metropolitan Museum of Art offers a special service to creators of fashion. From its treasury of ancient art, New York designers take many ideas.

And so it goes with everything else.

"What other *process* could be adapted to this job?" Questions like this have led to ideas that have raised America's standard of living. Likewise, the finding of the right machine often calls for exploring parallels. In the same way, tools meant for one purpose can be successfully adapted for something else.

"Out of whose book can I take a lead?" What is experience but a wealth of parallels upon which our imagination can draw? Nor does it have to be first-hand experience. Vicariously, our minister Dr. Butzer has lived hundreds of lives—lives in distress. He can counsel because he can take many leaves out of many books, and the right leaves. He knows what works and what fails in trying to rehabilitate a life. He knows what ideas to transplant from one case to another.

To step up our creative power we need to pile up alternatives. Whether for better writing, better music, better product, better process—or for a brighter life— let's pile up plenty of alternatives by way of parallels. Let's borrow ideas right and left and adapt them to our needs.

LET'S LOOK FOR A NEW TWIST; LET'S MODIFY

"What if this were somewhat changed?" "How can this be altered for the better?" "How about a new twist?"

No matter what our creative problem, let's ask ourselves, "How could we do this differently?" Even when we have to make a speech, we might well challenge every feature of our talk with that question.

"What change can we make in the process?"

"How about changing the *shape*?" "In what *way*?" "In what *other* ways?"

Roller-bearings go back to about 1500 and Leonardo da Vinci. For four centuries they were straight-sided cylinders, of less use than ball-bearings. The revolutionary improvement came in 1898 when Henry Timkin first patented his tapered roller-bearing. This entailed but a slight modification of shape in the cylinder type. But the new design took care of both radical and thrust loads, and thus surpassed all other forms of bearings.

"In what *form* could this be?" Sugar was first granulated, then powdered, then put into square lumps. Someone in the American Sugar Company then asked a shape question, "Wouldn't these dice-like lumps look more attractive if made into oblongs like dominoes?" Except when slowed down by war, Domino has grown stronger and stronger ever since.

"What *other* package?"

"What other changes can we make to provide more sense-appeals?" What would attract the eye and the ear, as well as the taste, the sense of touch and the sense of smell? "What color would be better?" "How about motion?" "What can we do with sound?"

What *else* can be modified, or given a new twist? And again, what *else*?

WHAT IF WE ADD, OR MULTIPLY; OR MAGNIFY?

"What strength can we *add*?" "How about extra *value*?" "Could this be *multiplied*?" Through *addition* we may arrive at an idea, only to find that its value depends upon thinking up a *new use*. Such was the case when Pittsburgh Plate sought a bigger volume in mirror-glass. The first idea was to sell larger mirrors. Fine, but where? A relatively new use was thought up and tried out—large mirrors to cover doors—and this turned out to be the answer.

In piling up alternatives through addition, we should go beyond size. "How about more time?" Many a process has been improved through longer aging.

Greater frequency may also be worth exploring, "What if this were done more often?"

"How could this be *reinforced*?" By heat-treating the rims of table glasses, Libby made a success of no-tick tumblers.

Size is the simplest key to ideas through magnification.

"How can I add *value*?"

When it comes to products, the plus of a new ingredient is often worthwhile.

What to add by way of a pleasant environment is a key question in employee relations.

"How about doubling it?" My friend John Oishei originally thought of only one windshield wiper to a car. He doubled the use—two wipers became standard equipment on each windshield. "Double Your Money Back" worked so well that advertisers have since copied the device.

Exaggeration can be a powerful club in driving home a point. Stan Hunt, who has drawn many comics for the *Saturday Evening Post*, admits that exaggeration is his best stock in trade.

Exaggeration is but one of the many byways which lead off from the magnification highway. By sending our imagination down these trails, we can add more alternatives; and the more numerous the alternatives, the better the ideas. In turn, the conscious effort we put into such quests tends to step up our creative power.

LET'S SUBTRACT AND DIVIDE; LET'S MINIFY

After having beaten the bushes of *more-so*, we should shift our hunt to *less-so*. "What if this were *smaller*?" "What could I *omit*?" "How about *dividing*?"

"Why don't we make it lighter?"

Time-saving is important. "Could this be faster?"

B.F. Goodrich created a new fire hose that is 18% lighter yet stronger; and because it is *lighter*, the hose can be put into action *faster*.

"What can we eliminate?" Elimination of the objectionable is an obvious creative challenge.

The factor of omission is often important in human relations. It is well to ask ourselves, "What could be left *unsaid*?" Such silence is often golden diplomacy, and certainly plays a big part in the everyday tact that helps to brighten our lives.

Let's also think of separating into *assortments*. This idea seems to work in the chicken business splitting up foul and selling legs to those who want legs.

The less-so trail and the more-so trail often cross each other. Arrow Shirts followed both and arrived at the idea of *fewer* pins and *larger* pins—each pin with a head so big that it obligingly sings out, "Here I am!"

LET'S SEEK "THAT" INSTEAD OF "THIS"; LET'S SUBSTITUTE

We're still piling up alternatives—still listing more and more what-else ideas. An obvious key to more what-elses is substitution. The change of this for that is not limited to things. Places, persons, and even emotions can be substituted.

Even ideas can be transferred. The classic example of this is the "eureka" story about Archimedes. He had to find out whether a crown was all gold. How to figure the cubic area of the crown was too much for him. So, as often helps in creative thinking, he took a hot bath. "My body makes the water rise. It displaces exactly the same cubic area. I will immerse the crown in water, measure how much it displaces, and thus find its cubic area. Multiplying that by the known weight of gold, I can then prove whether the crown is a counter-feit. *'Eureka.'*" I wasn't there at the time but I imagine that's how his mind worked when interchanging an idea by substituting water displacement for metal measurement.

Many worthwhile new ideas have come from seeking a *substitute component.*

"How about making parts *interchangeable?*"

Multi-use is another phase of interchangeability.

Let's also ask ourselves, "What other ingredient?" For many centuries, soap was soap. Then one improved soap after another was arrived at through substitution of ingredients. The newest idea is "soapless" soaps. These have come from the substitution of a new chemical compound known as fatty alcohol sulfates. Who would ever think of putting glue into a cleaning compound? Two Milwaukee men thought up and produced Spic and Span. Proctor and Gamble noted its meteoric success in the Midwest and paid the amateur chemists a fortune for their product.

In talking to a glue manufacturer, I found this to be the first time that glue was ever used as a cleaning ingredient. The animal glue industry had long been alarmed by the inroads of vegetable glues and synthetic glues. Their researchers had racked their brains as to what big new uses could be found for animal glue. Was the idea of its use for cleaning purposes too far-fetched to expect of them? Didn't they fail to shoot wild enough and to pick up enough new use alternatives for their creative thinking?

When Du Pont created nylon no one in the company would have predicted that it would one day be used to make zippers. The ingenuity of people in the Hookless Fastner Company, however, saw in nylon a superior substitute.

"What other *process*?" is another finding a question. Should it be roasted? Or should it be toasted? Or should it be steamed? Should it be processed in vacuum or under pressure? Should it be cast, or should it be stamped? These are but few of countless ways in which we can challenge a process to the end of a better idea.

"*Who* else?" In piling up alternatives through substitution, we might ask ourselves questions along that line.

"*Where* else?"

The substitution trail is an endless road to an infinite number of ideas. No matter what our problem, let's make our imagination go on the hunt in the many fields into which the road leads. But don't forget your pencil. And you'd better have a pencil-sharpener ready, too—you will find so many, *many* alternatives to write down.

LET'S CHANGE THE PATTERN; LET'S RE-ARRANGE

Re-arrangement usually offers an unbelievable quantity of alternatives. For instance, a baseball manager can shuffle his team's batting order 362,880 times.

"What about sequence?" Cafeterias found that desserts sell better when sold near the start of the line instead of at the end.

"What if they were transposed?" Even such questions of re-arrangement can be sources of ideas. One reason for this is that we do not always know what is cause and what is effect; we still are not sure which came first, the chicken or the egg.

It is well to think in terms of transposing cause and effect—of asking of an apparent effect, "Is this perhaps the cause?"—or asking of an alleged cause, "Is this perhaps the effect?" Many a person has given way to the alibi, "People don't like me—that is why I am morose and sensitive." If such grouches would try hard enough to be cheerful and objective instead of glum and subjective, the effect would probably be that people would like them.

"What about timing?"

"What about a change of pace?"

"What about schedules?"

Thousands of alternatives are lurking in the fields of re-arrangement. By sending our imaginations thither on the hunt, we can bag many an idea. This is only one of many ways in which we can step up our creative power.

THERE'S LOTS OF GOOD HUNTING
IN VICE VERSA

"What about the opposite?" and "What if this were reversed?" This topsy-turvy form of creativity is what Hollywood calls *switcheroo*. Many a movie plot has been thought up, or sparked up, by having the man bite the dog instead of *vice versa*.

Such creative thinking is based on a search for the opposite of the conventional, and Leo Nejelski has stressed the needs of this even in business executives.

"Many," he said, "have found that they get original ideas when they systematically challenge the obvious."

Thomas S. Olsen uses a slightly different version of reverse thinking. "When hunting for an idea," he told me, "I always go from the positive to the negative, and vice versa." By trying to first think of the obvious, then of opposites of the obvious, he uses an alternating current to step up his creative power.

Contrast is a cardinal principle of association. The more we try to think in reverse, the more we enlist the help of this automatic power of ours.

Another reverse twist is literally to turn things upside down. "Why not try it on the other end?" The nub of Howe's invention of the sewing machine was that instead of putting the eye of the needle at the end opposite the point, he put the eye at the point.

"How about building it upside down?" Through such reverse thinking, Henry Kaiser spectacularly sped up the construction of ships during the war. His idea was to build whole sections such as the deck-houses upside down, so that the welders could work downhand instead of overhead.

"Into whose shoes should I put myself?" can be a good business question. In talking of ideas, E. M.

Statler once told me: "I try never to look upon myself as a hotel proprietor, but always to put myself in the shoes of my guests. By thinking in terms of their wants, I have arrived at some of my best ideas." In competitive thinking, we might also do well to put the shoe on the other foot by asking ourselves: "What plus could he add which might put my product behind the eight-ball?"

The Albert Art Gallery encouraged good taste with a chamber of horrors. It was called *This is Bad Design*, being an exhibition to end exhibitions. The event attracted crowds for three afternoons and three evenings. The horrible examples consisted of household pieces so outlandish that their unique appeal had saved them from the scrap-heap. Completely irreconcilable with modern standards of good taste, most of the designs were monstrously mongrel. A critic described the collection as "the most incredible gingerbread that a preceding generation ever cooked up." Object lessons based on opposites hit home.

"How about doing the unexpected?" Years ago a Hollywood press-agent was asked to pinch hit for a friend as a commentator on a news-reel. One shot showed a baseball player coming to a sudden stop.

"Put screeching breaks under it," he called to the sound manager. When the reel was exhibited, movie patrons rolled in the aisles at the unexpected touch. From this idea, express agent Pete Smith went on to develop his series of comedy-shorts, and to establish a new school of sport comment. Some of his one-reelers made more money than successful full-length features.

There are so many little ways in which we can work via vice versa in our relations with each other. For example, a woman about to leave on a long trip gave each of her friends a "going-away" present. A daughter I know always gives presents to her mother and father on *her* birthday.

Unexpected kindliness can do wonders in business. It surprises me how many people believe that to get ahead in business they must grab and shove and call attention to themselves. In my own experience, the opposite has worked far better at every turn. The fact is that we serve ambition best when we bear in mind the old saying: "The average run of us fret and worry ourselves into nameless graves, while here and there a great unselfish soul forgets itself into immortality."

THREE

Imagination Guides

YOUR CREATIVE KEY MAY BE A COMBINATION

"What if this and that were put together?" Alloys have played a big part in our industrial progress. "Blended Fibers" is a term we hear of more and more. We took for granted that tubes and tires had to be separate.

Benjamin Franklin got tired of changing from one set of specs to another, so he cut his lenses in two and stuck them together with the reading halves below.

A big new idea was worked out by Edwin H. Land for consolidating a developing room with a camera.

Science creates largely by combination. Chemistry is mainly based on compounding. Horticulturists create new plants by grafting.

Well, there, in at least nine sections, we have guide upon guide to help us make the most of out imaginations. It all boils down to piling up alternatives in one way or another to the end that we have *plenty*—so many that among them there is a mathematical likelihood of our finding the ideas we seek. Even the *effort* invested will of itself step up our creative power.

IDEAS WILL FLY IN OUR WINDOWS, IF WE'VE OPENED THEM

Hurray! We can now relax. At this point we stop piling up alternatives and let our minds go blank in order that stray ideas—"butterflies," poet John Masefield called them—may be tempted to fly in through our mental windows. All creative thinkers pay homage to this phenomenon, which produces bright ideas so often that it is called *illumination*. Because of the *suddenness* of its flashes, it is also known as "the period of luminous surprise."

Although illumination is effortless, we sometimes need to use a bit of will-power to set the right climate for our butterflies and to shoo away their enemies. For instance, when I sit down for a haircut, I usually say to my friend the barber: "If you don't mind, Joe, I'd like to do a little thinking." But I don't really *try to think*, but rather to let myself *dream*. Usually, by the time the hot towel is pulled off my face, something by way of a sought-for idea will have mysteriously flown into my mind.

Such short snatches of illumination are like naps compared to a long sleep. After a sustained drive, we should coast far longer—long enough to brood, for brooding helps to woo an idea. Although Newton called this same process, "thinking of it all the time," he too, believed in periods of star-gazing between his spells of conscious training.

Many scientists have stressed illumination. Said Darwin is his autobiography, "I can remember the very spot in the road, whilst in my carriage, when to my joy the solution occurred to me." Hamilton, describing his discovery of equations, reported that his basic solution came to him as he "was walking with Lady Hamilton to Dublin, and came up to Brougham Bridge." But Darwin and Hamilton had put in years of deliberate thinking to reach those points of illumination.

In literature, the same phenomenon has been marveled at by Goethe, Coleridge and countless others, and often referred to figuratively. Stevenson spoke of his "Brownies" as helpers who worked for him while he slept. Barrie gave much credit to "McConnachie"— whom he described as "the unruly half of me, the writing half." Milton dubbed as "droughts" his periods of illumination. He actually courted these spells by just brooding over a theme and deliberately writing nothing. Sometimes in the night he would awaken his daughters and dictate poetry to them.

Modern authors have similarly attested. "A story must simmer in its own juice for months or even years before it is ready to serve," wrote Edna Ferber. A newer novelist, Constance Robertson, told me this: "I have found that it pays to hold a plot in suspension, and not to worry it or force it. At the right point, I go into a long lull. *Then,* I tackle my typewriter and write whatever comes. My story then seems to reel itself off in the most extraordinary way."

Illumination has been explained as "intellectual rhythm"; but that seems more poetic than expository. It has also been described as the "*subconscious* at work." But isn't this too general, and isn't the subconscious hypothetical?

A clearer psychological explanation was put forth by Elliot Dunlap Smith of Carnegie Tech in an address: "If the knowledge of the inventor and the clues which will bring the invention into being have been brought nearly into position to provide the inventive insight, his inner tension will be strong. As he nears his goal he will become increasingly excited. It is no wonder that the sudden release of such inner tension is often described as a 'flash.'"

Unconscious effort in the form of *inner tension* appears to be a most likely theory. But there may be other ways to explain illumination, and one of these has to do with motivation. Creative thinking thrives on enthusiasm, and this tends to lag when we force our minds beyond a creative point. By letting up a while, we tend to regenerate our emotional urge.

Another explanation is that our power of association often works best when running freely on its own. During time-out, this untiring helper is more likely to scurry around in the hidden corners of our minds and pick up the mysterious ingredients which combine into *ideas*.

Even a *psychological* explanation may lie in the fact that our gray-matter, as well as the rest of us, is subject to fatigue. The neuron is technically indicated as the basic unit of our nervous system, and the exertion of thinking calls upon these neurons to work upon each other. They, too, can do with rest-periods.

However, when all is said and done, illumination will probably remain a mystery like life itself.

As to how to woo illumination, one good rule is to take *enough time*; and a good way to do that is to *start sooner*. Monday is supposed to be my minister's day off, but he finds he can turn out a better sermon if he makes a good start on Monday instead of later. By spreading his creative work over a longer span, he gives illumination more chance to help. Henry Ward Beecher is said to have conceived every one of his sermons at least two weeks in advance of delivery.

We can sometimes induce illumination by deliberately *stopping* our conscious thinking. In my travels I ran across a story about a boxer named Beau Jack. It struck me that this might suit *The Reader's Digest*, so I got the facts and consciously tried to work up my narrative. When I failed to find the right angle, instead of forcing myself further, I dashed off the tale in a letter to my son and thus deliberately brushed it off my mind. Two days later, the needed idea came to me and I quickly wrote my manuscript almost exactly as published.

Sleep, above all else, helps court illumination, for it tends to unleash our power of association as well as to unweary our mind. While William Deininger was turning the General Baking Company from failure to success, I had free access to his office, even though I was less than half his age.

"My boy, do you know that I nap here now and then?" he asked me one day. I sheepishly confessed that I knew. "Well, my lad," he went on, "I want you to realize that those naps of mine are not wastes of time. I keep pondering a problem and don't get the answer. Then, if I feel like it, I doze off and when I wake up the solution is right there looking at me."

While naps may help, a good night's sleep will do more. But if we rush at it too hard on first arising, we may lose some good ideas. It is better to breakfast leisurely, or even to loaf a bit, and thus prevent premature pressure from nipping the buds of our nocturnal illumination.

Burdette Wright had to turn out more and more warplanes every day during the time when Hitler had our backs against the wall. I knew Mr. Wright and wondered how, with his mind so tortured by pressure, he could do the creative thinking his job demanded. So I asked one of his staff, Charles Augspurger, who told me this: "He would eat with us at noon, but very lightly, and then would lock himself in his office for an hour. During that time he would lie on a sofa and—as he later told me—would just dream with his eyes open. Almost every afternoon, after one of these siestas, Mr. Wright would bring into our conference at least one good idea he had thought of in his "do-nothing" period."

To cultivate illumination Lowell Thomas recommends a prescription from Yoga which calls for "a deliberate, sustained period of silence—just an hour of silence, sitting still, neither reading nor looking upon anything in particular."

Illumination can also be coaxed by shifting our minds to another subject. Psychologist Ernest Dichter has warned against staying too long with one task: "If you have difficulty in sticking to a certain goal, give in to your natural desire to change to something else. This is particularly important when you do creative work." Edison habitually switched from one project to another and worked on several simultaneously.

"Among the best ways to relax," said Dr. Suits of General Electric, "are hobbies, provided they are not taken too seriously. Mine are skiing and playing the clarinet. I have friends in the laboratory who botanize, collect Indian relics, study the stars. One business executive I know has discovered that his mind is more likely to be full of fresh ideas at the morning conference if he spends the evening fiddling with his ship models instead of pouring over the company reports."

For a year before Pearl Harbor, I worked from time to time with Admiral Nimitz. Even then, his problems were almost too much for anyone's mind; what a mental strain he must have been under when later directing the strategy of our fleets against the Japanese! One of my former associates, Nate Crabtree, was on his staff. "The Admiral would work feverishly and for long hours," Nate told me recently. "But he would take time out, morning, noon and night. Before breakfast he would take a hike, each morning he would practice for 15 minutes on our pistol range, once a week he would swim for at least a mile, and almost every day he would play tennis or pitch horseshoes."

Most creative advisors counsel us against diversion through reading while on a creative quest. Graham Wallas regarded passive reading as "the most dangerous substitute for bodily and mental relaxation during the stage of incubation."

Since there is something mystic about illumination, we might well relax in ways that can kindle the *spiritual* in us. When in 1697, William Congreve penned "Music has charms to soothe the savage beast . . ." he might have added that music also helps to woo the muse of illumination. Concerts are recommended. A record-changing phonograph is a good accessory. Pile up a dozen platters of good music without words, sit in your favorite chair and just listen. If, before this, you have put in enough steady effort on your creative problem, you may soon see "butterflies" circling around your living room.

An even more spiritual lull can be had in church. A friend who won success in real estate recently confessed to me that he can get more ideas there than anywhere else. Robert G. Le Tourneau, who climbed to the heights through his inventions of earth-moving apparatus, received an urgent order from the Army for a device to pick up shattered war-planes. He and his assistants went to work feverishly, but ran up against a stone wall. "I am going to a prayer-meeting tonight," he told them. "Perhaps the solution will come while I am there." Thus, as far as he could, he erased the problem from his conscious mind. Before the closing prayer, the picture of the wanted design suddenly flashed before him. He went home and made a working sketch of it that very night.

When ideas come through illumination, what should we do? Should we reach out and grasp them or should we sit back and do nothing? At least one authority on creative thinking recommends inaction, even to the point of restraining oneself from making the notation; but the weight of testimony seems to be on the side of those who favor action, even to the point of quickly pinning down the idea with a pencil. As witness in behalf of this policy, here are five who could well qualify as experts:

Physiologist R. W. Gerard of the University of Chicago advocated making notes of ideas, whenever and however they come, and cited this case: "Otto Loewi, recently awarded the Nobel Prize for proving that active chemicals are involved in the action of nerves, once told me the story of his discovery. His experiments on the control of a beating frog heart were giving puzzling results. He worried over these, slept fitfully and, lying wakeful one night, saw a wild possibility and the experiment would test it. He scribbled some notes and slept peacefully till next morning. The next day was agony—he could not read the scrawl nor recall the solution, even though remembering that he had had it. That night was even worse until at three in the morning lightning flashed again. He took no chances this time, but went to the laboratory at once and started his experiment.

Dr. Harry Hepner, head of psychology at Syracuse University, writing of illumination as the appearance of a "good idea seemingly from nowhere," expressed himself as strongly in favor of catching each gleam and caging it as it comes: "Failure to record the flash, or to follow it through, may entail a tragic inability to do so later," was his conclusion. And Yale's Professor of Philosophy, Brand Blanshard, added: "Seize the illuminations of the unconscious when they come. One should keep a notebook always ready to record them."

Graham Wallace testifies that many of his best ideas come to him while in his bathtub, and that he felt there was a great need for new creative tools in the form of waterproof pencils and waterproof notebooks.

Ralph Waldo Emerson put the case just as strongly: "Look sharply after your thoughts. They come unlooked for, like a new bird on your trees, and, if you turn to your usual task, disappear."

Illumination comes while coasting, but coasting inescapably implies that power has been previously applied. A tragic tendency of mental Micawbers is to overrate illumination and underrate effort. The fact is that the ideas we receive while idling are quite often by way of extra dividends.

One reason so much is made of brilliant flashes is that they can be dramatized, while the hard truth behind such flashes is usually dull. Charles Goodyear found a new way to make rubber useful, and did so while fooling around the kitchen stove. That's about all the public knows in regard to his discovery. Only a few realize how many years of hard work and sacrifice preceded his moment of triumph.

"Watt invented the steam-engine—he thought it up on a fine Sunday afternoon while taking a walk."

That is what most of us believe. How true is it? In the first place, he did not invent the engine—he invented a condenser which made steam power more widely usable. And what's the truth about Watt's Sunday flash? As a matter of history, he had not only been thinking of the problem, but working on it, for a long time before he took his historic walk.

Anthony Trollope railed against the notion that ideas "just grow" on the tree of illumination. Said he in his autobiography: "There are those who think that people who work with their imaginations should wait till inspiration strikes. When I have heard this doctrine preached, I have scarcely been able to repress my scorn."

The neatest summary of the cold truth about illumination was written by Henry Poincaré: "This unconscious work is not possible, or in any case not fruitful, unless it is first preceded and then followed by a period of conscious work."

"Butterflies" are likely to come to us willy-nilly, but far more so when we have opened our windows by means of conscious preparation. The more alternatives we have piled up, the more and better butterflies will fly our way during our illuminative periods.

LADY LUCK SMILES UPON THOSE
WHO ARE 'A-HUNTING'

The distinction between illumination and inspiration, according to Dr. William Easton, is this: *Illumination* wells up from unknown sources, whereas almost every creative *inspiration* arises from "an accidental stimulus" which can be clearly traced. Another difference is that illumination mostly comes from what the *past* has put into our minds, whereas inspiration usually comes from something that happens in the present. Then, too, illumination has to do with ideas which come to us while idling, whereas the luck of inspiration may strike us either while driving hard or while coasting.

But enough for academic difference. The practical questions are: "How and when do these accidents happen?" "What should we do about them?"

Let's first dispose of sheer accidents. The discovery of coal in America was an out-and-out accident. A Pennsylvanian hunting in the mountains built his campfire on an outcropping ledge of black rocks and was amazed when they caught fire and burned.

The discovery of iron in Minnesota was far less of an "accident." The seven Merritt brothers had long tramped the Mesabi Range, convinced by the vagaries of their compasses that worlds of ore lay hidden there. When their wagon mired down in rusty red mud, they found the iron.

Just "getting around" tends to court Lady Luck. Wagner was always thinking of new ideas for operas; and yet, if he hadn't gone to sea and ridden through a storm, he might never have thought of *The Flying Dutchmen*.

Luck does most for those bent on a specific search. Frank Clark, a G.E. engineer, could have been reading the comics on a certain evening; but his mind was on a certain hunt. So instead of loafing he leafed through a technical publication. A word leaped up and hit him in the eye. "That's it!" he exclaimed. It was "diphenyl," which turned out to be the missing link in his search of a way to prevent short circuits in power line transformers.

And how about Madame Curie and her husband— how did they "stumble upon" radium? What happened was that Madame Curie's thesis for a doctor's degree dealt with the problem of why uranium seemed to shed light-rays. Her husband joined her in the search and at long last they "accidentally" got on the trail of "radium." Whatever luck the Curies had came from unswerving perseverance.

The son of Elmer Sperry put to him this question: "Daddy, why does a top stand up when it spins?" That chance remark helped lead Sperry to his invention of the Gyro-compass which revolutionized navigation. Wasn't it lucky that Sperry knew enough to recognize and to adapt that accidental suggestion?

Accidents are seldom the answers. Good breaks count most in what they lead to—if we follow through. A Dutch naturalist named Swammerdam had observed the same frog-leg accident long before Galvani did; but Swammerdam never followed up his observation. On the other hand, that twitching electrified Galvani into action.

"Whereupon," wrote Galvani, "I was inflamed with an incredible zeal and eagerness to test the same and to bring to light what was concealed in it."

As in piling up alternatives, we have in accidents the benefit law of probabilities which academic logic makes much of, but which seems to boil down to the fact that the more we fish, the more likely we are to get a strike. As Matthew Thompson McClure has told us, the idea that comes "as a flash" usually comes to the one who is experimenting with the problem.

"Some people deliberately hunt for inspiration," said Dr. William Easton, "as one hunts for game. They go where they are likely to find it; they keep constantly on the alert for it. Although inspiration is uncontrollable, the chances that it will occur can be increased by enlarging the stock of ideas in the mind and by multiplying observation."

Yes, in creative effort we can largely make our own lucky breaks; we can help inspire our own inspirations. Here again quantity attracts quality. It's the same in sports. The more we swing for the fence, the more likely we are to homer.

MOST IDEAS ARE STEP-BY-STEP CHILDREN OF OTHER IDEAS

The story of ice cream well illustrates this step-by-step process, for it covers a span of over 1,800 years. Mrs. McCabe's flavored snowball was new to her, and yet the same concoction was served by Nero in 62 A.D. To celebrate a gladiatorial contest, he rushed runners from Rome to the mountain-tops and had them bring back snow which Nero's cooks flavored with honey.

History loses track of ice cream until about 12 centuries later, when Marco Polo brought a startling new recipe from Asia to Rome—a kind of dessert just like Nero's ices. Two centuries later, the Medicis made a hit by climaxing their feasts with what Catherine called "fruit-ice."

In the 17th century, King Charles I paid 500 pounds to a French chef to make ice cream for the royal table; but the chef kept his recipe a secret.

The idea of ice cream came out in the open about 1707 when the New York *Gazette* ran advertisements announcing our first ice-cream parlors. George Washington is said to have bought ice cream from one of these New York shops around the corner from where he lived when he was President of the United States.

Dolly Madison made ice cream in the White House entirely by hand. The new idea of a crankable ice cream freeze was the brain child of Nancy Johnson just about 100 years ago.

And so it went, improvement after improvement, one new idea on top of another—until came Eskimo Pie, and now a ready-prepared sundae in a paper box with the chocolate syrup frozen right over the ice cream! What next?

This history of ice cream not only illustrates the step-by-step process and the long lapses between ideas on a given subject, but also illustrates how often someone thinks up something "new" without knowing that someone, somewhere else in the world, has thought up almost the same idea.

Sometimes we may have the seed of an idea, but fail to make it grow. Near a southwest hamlet, I saw a group of people in a vacant lot, and, being curious, joined the crowd. The magnet was a photographer who, for 25 cents, would take your picture while you sat on a 1,000-lb. steer. He pointed his black box at me, clicked a shutter, fumbled around in the box, and in about a minute handed me my finished photo. His name was Russel Chamberlain. He had been taking pictures all over the West for 22 years with that all-inclusive camera, which he had made for himself out of an old lunch box. Although his product was a tin-type, I couldn't help but think: "What if Russel Chamberlain had not stopped with his creation of that one crude device, but had gone on in search of the similar, but far superior, all-in-one camera developed and perfected 16 years later by Polaroid scientists?"

An idea can be ahead of its time, like Leon Forcault's Gyroscope. He worked this out in 1852 to demonstrate the rotation of the earth. When Robert Thompson thought up pneumatic tires in 1845 it was a case of "so what?"

There were practically no improvements on recipes for generations, until Fanny Farmer added one new and important idea. Before her time all recipes had read, "Take a heaping teaspoon full." (How much is heaping?) "Season to taste," etc. Fanny changed that to: "Take two level teaspoonfuls." "Season with seven drops of vanilla."

In view of all this, we should not be too quick to reject any of our ideas as too trivial. Above all, we should think up other uses we could make of them. Steam was used in Egypt in 120 B.C.—but only to spin a toy.

The biggest lesson we can learn from the step-by-step nature of ideas is that we can never stop improving. One day on the way to the General Motors Research Laboratory I passed a group of abandoned buildings and asked what they were. "There," said my Dayton friend, "is where the great firm of Barney and Smith used to make most of the world's railroad cars. When steel cars started, they stood firm in their belief that wooden cars were better. That's why they went up the flue."

Remember Pierce Arrow? Along about 1910 that was the best-known car and known to be the best car. At one time just those two words "Pierce Arrow" could easily have sold for at least a million. But while competitors were innovating one idea after another to make cars better and cheaper, Pierce Arrow engineering stood still creatively. Just before the company's end, I was authorized to try to sell the name. I went to Detroit and did my best; but by that time, no other car manufacturer wanted those two words at any price.

These last 16 chapters have outlined basic procedure. Before we leave this part of our subject, let's take a look at the final and often indispensable step—*backtracking*.

When stumped in the course of a creative project, we need to stop and review. We should analyze the problem anew, should think up still other alternatives, and then proceed all over again.

When at the end of a creative project, we find we have failed, it usually pays to reprocess from start to finish. If we have met with seeming success in our creative pursuit, we should then replace imagination with judgment. But let's beware of *perfectionitis*. A fair idea put to use is better than a good idea kept on the polishing wheel.

TWO HEADS ARE BETTER THAN ONE; BUT NOT ALWAYS

How can we work best creatively—singly, in teams or in groups? Since now, as never before, so many of the best ideas come out of research staffs, let's first glance at this highly organized method of harnessing power.

Scientific research started only a few centuries ago. The early investigators, according to Dr. James Conant, were "lone workers." Then some of these amateurs began to collaborate, or rather cooperate, in "scientific societies." In 1651 several Italians banded together and later founded the *Accademia del Cimento*, which outshone the British Royal Society of that day in both brilliance and continual effort.

That kind of loose organization was about all there was until about the turn of the century when organized research, as we now know it, came into being; and in this century such research has grown to be the fountainhead of most new ideas.

Despite such advances in organized research, the creative power of the individual is what still counts the most. To the far-flung research staffs of Du Pont, Dr. Ernest Benger has spelled out his philosophy: "No idea has ever been generated except in a single human mind. No matter how you toss this thought around or how you add to it by consideration of the effect of getting people into a coordinated organization, the fact still remains that every idea is the product of a single brain."

Creative history sparkles with the names of solitary thinker-uppers. Just as there are those who temperamentally do their best creative work by themselves, others have to work on their own through the very nature of their calling. Ministers are among them. Sheer circumstance sometimes forces us to think up by our lonesome. Robinson Crusoe was the peerless exemplar of this.

Many of us work much better creatively when teamed up with the right partner. In business, a sparkplug and a brake may make a good team. Such are Hull and Dobbs of Memphis, who built two great food chains, sell more Ford cars than any other dealer in the world, and supply 14 airlines with daily meals. One is a salesman. The other is precise, thorough—an engineer. The salesman Dobbs incubates endless ideas. He will fire at any target that moves. Hull sits still, analyzes and censors. He will not fire without a range-finder, double-checked.

A famous trio in General Electric originated a complete line of alternating-current equipment, announced and advertised as the "SKC" system—Stanley, Kelly, Chesney. They were an aggressive triumvirate, and their work greatly accelerated the development of the alternating current.

However, there is a danger. The more faith one has in team-mate(s), the more the instinct is likely to say: "What's the use of my trying too hard? They will think up the answer." This hazard of teamwork can be avoided by simple procedures. For one thing, during certain periods in a creative quest, each member of a team should go off by themselves and do some brainstorming on their own. When the partners come together after such solo thinking, they will find that they have piled up more worthwhile alternatives than if they had kept on working as one all the time.

Then, too, it is sometimes well for two teammates deliberately to change roles. At one time let "A" act as creator and "B" as critic. At another time let "B" be the one who shoots wild, with the other acting as judge. But even in such a change-about we should always beware lest we judge prematurely—we should hold back criticism until the creative current has had every chance to flow.

HOW TO ORGANIZE TO CREATE IDEAS

Can a group produce ideas? The answer is yes. Properly organized and run, a group can be a gold mine of ideas.

It was in 1939 when I first organized such group-thinking in our company. The early participants dubbed out efforts *"Brainstorm Sessions"*; and quite aptly so because, in this case, "brainstorm" means using the brain to storm a creative problem—and do so in commando fashion, with each stormer attacking the same objective.

Judicial thinking must be kept out of such brainstorming. Even discretion is unwanted. As one of our participants remarked: "At any brainstorming table the villain is Prudence." In this operation all present must shoot wild and pile up every possible alternative by way of ideas.

Hundreds of such brainstorm sessions have been held in our offices and nearly all have been worthwhile in terms of ideas produced. The few fiascoes have been due to failure of leadership. If a group-chairperson displays omniscience, the more timid members are afraid to open their mouths, and others say to themselves: "All right, *you* know much better about it, *you* think up ideas." Leaders who allow criticism to creep into the proceedings likewise fail to get the best out of their brainstormers.

The conventional conference over-emphasizes judicial thinking, and almost ignores creative thinking. Most conferences are non-creative. Their usual purpose is to consider whether this is better than that; and such juries work well because we all love the role of critic. Truly creative conferences are not only rare, but likely to be abortive. Jim wants to impress, so he talks big and echoes: "In other words . . ." But he springs no ideas of his own. Jane hangs back until someone suggests: "Why not do so-and-so . . .?" And then Jane proceeds with: "That's interesting, but it won't work . . . You don't understand the facts . . ." Jane offers no ideas of her own.

How big should a brainstorming group be? The ideal number is between 5 and 10. Who should be involved? The less experienced sometimes spark better; but the ideal group should include both brass and rookies. At least two of the group should be self-starters, and they should begin sparking the moment the problem is stated.

In our business, it is relatively easy to conduct brainstorm sessions. I found it far tougher when I organized a volunteer group of the brightest young executives in our community to brainstorm civic problems.

"You know, it was hard to get through my head what you were trying to do with us. My 15 years of conference after conference in my company have conditioned me against shooting wild. Almost all of us officers rate each other on the basis of *judgment*—we are far more apt to look up to the other fellow if he makes but few mistakes than if he suggests lots of ideas. So I've kept myself from spouting any suggestions that my associates might sneer at. I wish our people would feel free to shoot ideas the way we have been doing in these brainstorm sessions."

What subjects lend themselves best to this kind of brainstorming? The first rule is that the problem should be specific rather than general.

A client wanted ideas on a name, a package and an introductory plan for a new product. We made the mistake of trying to brainstorm this multiple problem. Soon after our session started, one of us suggested a few names. We were just beginning to click with still more, when someone suggested a packing idea. Before we built up momentum along that line, someone switched us to marketing ideas. The session was a flop. We decided never again to tackle a complex subject in group brainstorming.

Initial goal statements can be much briefer for creative conferences than for judicial conferences. Facts are the brick and mortar out of which judgments are built; but in creative thinking, facts serve mainly as springboards. Too many facts can stifle the spontaneity needed in group brainstorming.

Group brainstorming needs a few simple ground rules, and the leader must make sure that these are understood by all present. So, in addition to outlining the problem, the leader should explain at the start:

1. *Judicial judgment* is ruled out. Criticism of ideas will be withheld until the next day.
2. *"Wildness" is welcomed.* The crazier the idea, the better; it's easier to tone down than to think up.
3. *Quantity is wanted.* The more ideas we pile up, the more likelihood of winners.
4. *Combination and improvement are sought.* In addition to contributing ideas of our own, let's suggest how another's idea can be turned into a better idea; or how two or more ideas can be joined into still another idea.

Those are the guides. The leader should put them into their own words because a brainstorm session should always be kept informal.

A few incurable critics will disregard the no criticism rule and will belittle what others suggest. At first, such a transgressor should be gently warned; but if they persist, they should be firmly stopped. In one of our sessions, when one participant kept on criticizing, the leader blasted him with: "If I were less vulgar, I might say, 'We don't want your opinions at this time.' What I do say is, 'Think up, or shut up!'"

The only strictly formal feature should be a written record of all ideas suggested. This list should be reportorial rather than stenographic.

The spirit of a brainstorm session can make or break it. Self-encouragement is needed almost as much as mutual encouragement. "When I can make my brainstorming team feel they are playing a game, we get somewhere," said one of our most successful leaders. The proof of a good brainstorm session is the number of ideas produced and the way the participants feel afterward. Why is group brainstorming productive? The main reason is that it concentrates solely on creative thinking and excludes the discouragement and criticism which so often cramp imagination. Another reason is contagion.

A psychological factor in group thinking is academically known as *social-facilitation*, a principle that has been proved by many scientific experiments. Experiments have proved that "free associations" on the part of adults are from 65 to 93 percent more numerous in group activity than when working alone.

This fact was confirmed by the Human Engineering
Laboratory of Stevens Institute.

In addition to producing rafts of ideas, such joint
ventures in thinking up do something for those who
take part. They gain in creative power. They see proof
that they can spark if they will. They get baptized into
a habit which can help them in private life as well as in
business.

IDEA-THINKING ON A LARGER SCALE; SUGGESTION SYSTEMS

Suggestion systems loom larger and larger as a creative
leaven for our nation. In 1880, in Scotland, ship-
builder William Denny originated the idea of asking
employees for ideas. His plan consisted of a wooden
box into which his workers were invited to drop suggestions for building better ships at less cost. That
box was the great-grandaddy of the many thousands
of similar boxes now found in American factories and
offices.

The first full-fledged suggestion system in the
United States was installed by the Navy in 1918.

There followed many others; but of all the suggestion plans installed in American industries prior to 1940, only about one out of 10 kept going. The mortality rate was high mainly because top management had not yet learned how to run idea systems. Too many sat back and hoped for some million-dollar ideas. No wonder their "plans" petered out.

It took World War II to put new life into the suggestion system movement. If properly run and adequately promoted, suggestion systems can do much to keep American business going strong.

Americans are supposed to excel in ingenuity. The environmental influences which make us creative are fast vanishing. This loss is being partly offset by the suggestion systems which are now stimulating the creative power of millions of individuals in the companies where idea plans are now on the march.

CREATIVE POWER NEEDS MORE HELP FROM EDUCATION

Our environment tends to sap the creative power of all of us except the few who use ingenuity in their daily work, as in the arts and in the creative phases of science and business.

To offset that blight, couldn't we do more to give our students a new concept? If education were to adopt a new concept of the importance of creative power, our colleges would need more clearly to distinguish between planting knowledge and training the mind. Tradition has tended to over-emphasize knowledge. We should recognize that knowledge is not power if made up merely of "inert facts" instead of active fuel for he mind. We should put *understanding* above *knowledge* in every field of study. Any such emphasis cannot help but play up principles and ideas rather than inert content. And this meets the specification laid down by writer Anatole France: "Let our teaching be full of *ideas*. Hitherto it has been stuffed only with facts."

Surely education should give elbow-room to imagination. Perhaps it might well go so far as to glorify imagination. A new and more dynamic concept might well recognize that only creative imagination can give wings to education.

Elliot Dunlap Smith of Carnegie Tech has proposed more creative projects *outside* the curriculum: "Students should be assigned creative problems outside of their customary field of work. Such an alien approach, as it so often has with great inventions, may provide a suggestive setting."

Many of us got most of our creative training from extracurricular activities while in college. My own creative effort was stepped up by editing the college newspaper, by writing short stories and "poetry" for the literary magazine edited by my classmate, Alexander Woollcott—and by working with Woollcott in organizing a dramatic group, still known as the "Charlatans." Surely such activities should be encouraged by educators. And every effort should be made to expand them.

To induce creativity, educators should do their best to arouse enthusiasm for imaginative thinking, to encourage every creative effort on the part of their pupils, to act as creative coaches. And, the more imagination they pack into their work, the more effective they are. O.C. Carmichael, head of the Carnegie Foundation for the Advancement of Teaching, has concluded that "the imaginative teacher is the ablest teacher."

By devoting more time and effort to the student's creative mind, the good teacher can also get more out of the creative life. For, as Cowling and Davidson put it, "in the cultivation of creative power lies the greatest joy of the teacher and the greatest hope for a better world."

CREATIVE POWER'S PLACE IN LEADERSHIP

"Creative thinking underlies resourceful leadership," said Elliot Dunlap Smith, and countless others attest to the same truth. The logic of it is that a leader must be versatile, possess judicial judgment to a marked degree, but not be solely judge, and must at least know their way around creativity. A leader will need to recognize the value of creativity, and to know how to tap and encourage the creative power of their associates.

"The ability to approach each problem with cold objective analysis is essential for success as an executive," said Richard Fear of the Psychological Corporation. Yes, but even decisions—especially if difficult—call for creative power.

What do we do to decide? First, we get all the facts, and list the pros and cons; but to do this well we also have to reach for the unknown—we have to guide our creative minds through the maze of *what-would-happen-if?* More often than not, a remote contingency, foreseen by imagination, turns out to be the determining factor.

To keep their feet on the ground a leader needs *precautionary judgment*, and this likewise calls for *anticipative imagination*. One of the ablest executives I know recently said to his board of directors: "We're sailing along fine but we ought to be on the lookout for rocks ahead. I made up a list of 20 things that might wreck us. Here they are." Later, he enlisted the help of five creative people with business experience and worked out a check-list of 179 such hazards.

Such vision must likewise be applied to positive questions of policy. More than one business has gone on the rocks through too much reliance on slide-rule judgment and too little use of anticipative imagination.

Too many big business executives tend to peter out creatively. They are not driven by sink-or-swim goals as in a little business; the sense of security in a large company tends to induce a "play-safe" policy. "Why should I try to think up ideas? Some of them would look screwy and might give me a black eye. In an organization as big as this, nobody will notice if I don't offer any suggestions, so to hell with ingenuity!"

Big business also offers so many *props* by way of analysis, surveys, and other studies; and props, whether for arches or for brains, weaken us when we lean on them too much. With fewer props, a small business is more likely to force each executive to keep up his creative power.

Every business, big or little, needs spark plugs— leaders who have ideas and know how to make them click. In large concerns, the ideal top executive doubles in brass as a creative pace-setter and a creative coach. They cultivate the creativity of those around them and make it bloom despite the stunting climate of magnitude. Above all else, leaders must feel a real regard for ideas. They cannot be like one I know who made a name for himself in the war despite his habit of looking down his nose and saying, "Ideas are a dime a dozen." Instead, a leader must be like John Collyer, who, according to his Research Director, Dr. Fritz, "not only welcomes every possible idea but makes us all feel that what he wants most from us is utmost use of our creative imagination."

Like trees, businesses tend to die from the top down, for the reason that the founders, as they grow older, sometimes tend to keep younger associates from trying their creative wings. An outstanding exception is Clare Francis of General Foods. "Younger executives come to me with what they think are new ideas," said Mr. Francis. "Out of my experience I could tell them why their ideas will not succeed. Instead of talking them out of their ideas, I have suggested that they be tried out in test areas in order to minimize losses. The joke of it is that half of these youthful ideas, which I might have nipped in the bud, turn out either to be successful or to lead to other ideas that are successful. The point I had overlooked was that while the idea was not new, the conditions under which the idea was to be carried out were materially different."

One of the needs of big business is to bring up the creative power of second-line executives. They sit in plenty of conferences, but these too often tend to cripple rather than to strengthen creative power. The younger conferees too often use their imaginations merely to anticipate how their associates will react; then, too, the conference-subjects usually call for judicial rather than creative thinking.

Although many businesses now have suggestion systems to gather creative contributions from employees, far less is done to stimulate ideas from associate executives. More of this might be achieved through group brainstorming, as set forth in a previous chapter.

Not only in business but in every line, the quality of leadership depends on creative power!

The Beginning . . .